Places of Rootedness

JESSIN KABIR

PLACES OF ROOTEDNESS

Author, editor and publisher: Jessin Kabir

Cover design: Jessin Kabir (Assisted by Gemini AI)

First Edition May 2026

Paperback ISBN: 978-93-5777-950-0

Email: contact.jessinkabir@gmail.com

CONTENTS

ACKNOWLEDGEMENTS

Apart from the places, there are a lot of faces to which I feel deeply rooted and connected.

I thank all my dear teachers and mentors from my school days who encouraged me to use a paintbrush and pen with efficiency and ease, and gave me the freedom to express my views and ideas through paintings and writings.

I express my gratitude to Children's Academy and its founder, Shri. P. Venugopal, who dedicated his life to nurturing new talents and promoting innovative ideas, and my first Art teacher, Artist Soman Sir, for introducing me to the basics of watercolour painting and the beauty of ordinary frames. The training I received in comprehensive writing during high school helped me excel in various literary competitions. And I truly enjoyed writing the language papers, which were like pieces of cake back then.

As a crowning touch, the art of systematic writing was introduced to me by my mentor, teacher, and well-wisher, (late) Dr S. Rajasekhar. He was the backbone of all my great endeavours and fortunes. His guidance helped me acquire both the prestigious milestones I have reached and the personal qualities that make me a better person. He was a voracious reader and was skilled in writing and public speaking. He generously lent me books from his personal collection, which helped me enrich my thoughts and ideas. His criticisms were inspirational in streamlining my work, including this one, and also in helping me find a niche in the world of writing. The light that he brought to my life will continue to guide me even in his absence.

Pursuing architecture for undergraduate and postgraduate studies at prestigious institutions helped me explore a lot of places and refine my writing. I cherish the wonderful experiences gained from my alma maters: the College of Engineering Trivandrum and the School of Planning and Architecture, New Delhi. My interactions with peers, faculty, and scholars, of multitude talents have been influential throughout my life.

Emotions and experiences, when attached to words, help them emerge as powerful tools to articulate the flow of thoughts. Writing is a powerful medium for expressing oneself. My writing was strengthened in the environs of Delhi while doing my Masters. In the 'Writing and Oral Skills' class, my teacher, Ms. Jeyanthi Natesalingam, asked us to write a character sketch of anyone we had seen in Varanasi, as Varanasi was the studio project for that semester. The next day, standing in front of the class, with my friends and teacher listening intently, I read out the character sketch of a *Dosa-wala* in Varanasi. The moment I stopped reading, one of my classmates raised her hands and clapped, shaking her head with her eyes closed and a smile of approval on her lips. My teacher joined her. Later, the entire class followed. That was the decisive moment when I realized that there was something in my writing. My dear friend and classmate at SPA, Ar. Sneha Borate from Mumbai encouraged my affinity for travel and writing travelogues. I thank all my other friends and well-wishers who have contributed to discovering and fine-tuning my literary skills and have helped me find places which I hold so dear to my heart.

Places of Rootedness is the product of my parents' encouragement and aspirations as well. Their broad-mindedness allowed me the freedom to travel and explore places far beyond their direct care and watchful eyes. My mother would patiently listen as the young version of me narrated everyday happenings, whether at home or at school. This habit of mine continued to grow with me. However, sometimes, for one reason or another, I could not explain everything to her, which bothered me a lot. I kept those remaining untold snippets on the safest shelves of my memory. And whenever I got time, I used to recollect them, both spatially and temporally, and structure them properly, so that I could present them to her when the right time came. The way I write is the way I narrate my life experiences to my mother.

It took ten years to complete this book, with the first draft starting in 2016. I am forever grateful for the immanent force within me that kept me going

INTRODUCTION

Once, during a train journey from Thane to Coimbatore, I met a young man named Noor, who was working in Mumbai. Knowing that I am from Kerala, he switched to a bilingual mix of Tamil and Malayalam. He was based in the northern part of Tamil Nadu, where his small family of four lived: his wife and two children. He was not happy with his life in the metropolis and always wanted to settle down in a rural setting in his hometown. And thus, with all his savings, he bought a piece of land in his native place for cultivation and to run a cattle farm. As he spoke, it drizzled outside, and raindrops quickly filled the window grilles. Pulling down the windowpane, he paused his story for a while and gazed at the view outside. The motion picture framed by the window showed the picturesque view of the farm fields, cattle and mountains of the Konkan. Seeing him diving into silent thoughts, I wondered if that was the kind of place he wanted to turn his little piece of land into.

After a while, he resumed talking and told me how people are treating their Mother Earth nowadays. The discussion went on to the concerns and issues raised by climate change. He took a deep sigh and told me, "Mountains are the nails on earth. Disturbing them will cause the loss of the whole equilibrium." I was really struck by how his poetic words conveyed such deep scientific thoughts. He was not a 'well-educated' person by our system's standards; even so, his knowledge of living in harmony with nature showed a concern for sustainable development that many of today's educated crowd are either unaware of or fail to practice. Noor stated that for living beings to connect with a place, the place must first be well-connected in space by retaining its original essential attributes.

Sneha, my classmate at SPA, was accompanying me on the same train journey. She was listening to our conversation as a mute spectator, being foreign to our language. I told her about Noor's dream of settling down in his hometown, leaving the city of Mumbai forever. Her response was quite contrary to Noor's, and she expressed her strong disapproval of people who complain about city life. Having been associated with Mumbai, she had another version to talk about that city. According to her, people from rural areas or suburbs migrate to cities for a living, and they take advantage of its infrastructure and gain everything from it—better education, jobs, improved facilities, etc. And yet, they later complain about the side-effects of urban life, such as pollution, traffic, land shortages, and congestion. She was indirectly mentioning the value of being thankful to the entities that have made us who we are today.

One evening, at her home in Thane, a couple of days before this train journey, I had seen her spending a lot of time looking out of the window of her bedroom. She slid open the windowpane and sat on its sill. The window frame was dotted with droplets left by the heavy rain during the Southwest monsoon. She was eagerly watching the views of the rain-soaked busy areas in Thane: the railway station, footbridge, apartments, shops, streets, vehicles, people moving around, and the grey rain clouds ready to shower again at any time. Whenever she opened that window, I could see the same enthusiasm in her eyes; it resembled a kid's, eager to explore something anew every moment.

Noor and Sneha are just two examples. Though both had roots in rural areas, they stood at opposite poles. Their affiliations and associations with places differed. Any place would offer the same thing to different people at any time. Yet, it is the memories and experiences created there that determine whether that place can foster a sense of belonging in people. At first glance, both of them might sound different. However, looking closer, one finds they were on the same page, showing love and gratitude for the places they belonged to and the tranquility they found—whether in the order or the chaos those places provided. They both accepted and praised the way places presented themselves to them, and just wanted those characteristics to be conserved, as they placed great value on their dearest places and the services they provided.

A place is not a singular, independent entity. The nature in its various manifestations, built enclosures of many sorts, people of extremely different character and characteristics, and the activities resulting from the interactions of all these member components together create a place that has plurality and interdependency at its core. A place enriches and enlivens our lives. It is a multi-dimensional whole that accumulates, organizes, and disseminates energy. Thus, a place becomes an inevitable, inseparable, and significant part of our memories and dreams.

I believe the spiritual being in humans has its energy dissipated in various places, sometimes remote in time and distance. And once that energy gets activated, its magnetic power pulls us towards it; our physical state (body) being drawn by the spiritual state (soul). Some places, even though kilometres away from our home, appear to be so near to us, primarily because of their nearness and dearness to our hearts. I have often been to places that had previously appeared in my dreams, have been to places that I had always wanted to see, and have been able to associate myself with some places instantaneously. And I believe that my soul has some connection with such places; a feeling of rootedness.

Sometimes, we find places that suit our needs, and sometimes, we create places as per our needs. Either way, humans have an innate nature to root themselves somewhere on this planet Earth. *Places of Rootedness* is a narrative of the places I have visited, how I familiarized myself with them, how I created my own world within them, and how I became deeply rooted; in essence, an autobiographical travelogue.

1 ECOSYSTEM OF MY HOME

It sounded wonderful when my mother walked with her slippers on the gravel-covered sloping path, carrying me in her arms. Her slippers would suppress, crush and then scatter the small stones and sand on the two-foot-wide pathway in the backyard of our home. The toddler in me used to wonder, "Would it sound the same if I were wearing my slippers?" Passing through the cycle of life, I too walked, and my slippers scattered the stones and sand on their way, and yet I could never recreate the rhythmic sound which I had listened to as a toddler.

My home and its environs are the places that anchor me to this world. No one who visited our home ever left without saying the word, "Greenness!" I could see the 'greenness' that they had perceived, mirrored in their sparkling eyes as well. To me, it is a 'little Amazon'! To our neighbours, our 'little Amazon' is a 'rainforest' that modifies the microclimate in the neighbourhood and a one-stop destination for things they may seek.

The floral wealth comprises tall coconut trees, tapioca, plantain, fruit trees of jackfruit, mango, chikoo, guava, custard apple, gooseberry, rambutan, mangosteen, Barbados/ West Indian cherry, Surinam cherry, Carissa carandas, pineapple shrubs, flowering plants like *Cassia fistula*, hibiscus, roses, *Asoka*

(Saraca asoca), jasmine, lily, henna, and the medicinal plants and creepers planted by my grandma. Accidental discoveries of new plants always surprised me. Once I ran home, screaming, "We have a *manchadi* tree (red lucky seed tree) here at our home!"

The faunal wealth includes daily visitors like crows, mynahs, parrots, hummingbirds and bats; pigeons, long-tailed birds and storks that come once in a while; peacocks and monkeys that come as a surprise from the forest around fifty kilometres away; squirrels, mongooses, snakes, frogs, and a few dogs and cats who come daily for food, and their companions who might follow in search of food and shelter, or perhaps even a fight. No one bought them, caged them, or put them in chains. They would come near us confidently and fearlessly. The only things extended to them are food, water, shelter, and above all, love. Among them, there have been a few favourites of my parents. Once, our neighbour's little goat 'Umer', saw us having lunch, broke his rope, and ran to my mother. He then occupied her lap and had a fistful of her meal. A black-coloured cat that had befriended my father used to follow him on his way back home and would saunter through the door with a cool attitude to sit beneath my father's bed, as if it were his 'black cat' security guard. Frictions occurred between them as well. He refused to acknowledge the cat the day it preyed on a squirrel and a mynah, ignoring his stern warnings while it was giving chase. Though differences exist, they in no way break the bonds of love and compassion towards our co-beings.

Little kids, on their way home from school and tuition, take a detour to visit our 'little Amazon', which to them is a bountiful grove offering a variety of exotic fruits and berries.

Different beings interpret the 'ecosystem' of my home in different ways: for my family, it is our world, our everything; for the animals, it is their 'mini' habitat; for the birds, it is a source of fruits and nectar-bearing flowers; for the kids, it is an orchard of indigenous and exotic fruits; for urban dwellers, it is an oasis!

My observations and explorations of nature began here, examining seasonal transitions, forecasting natural events like rain and storms, observing processes and life cycles such as flowering and fruiting, deciphering bird communication and their warnings of danger, understanding the social bonds among animals and birds, and so on. It is here that I learnt the art of growing plants, climbing trees, and tilling the soil with a spade. This is where I understood the beauty of living with compassion. John Ruskin, the 19th century polymath and art critic, believed that perfect beauty resides in God, and is reflected in nature, and that the master artist or craftsman, in turn, captures and imbibes this beauty into their medium of expression to produce great works. This is where I got the inspiration to draw, to paint, to sculpt, and to write. My parents recall that the first thing I ever scribbled was a parrot, drawn in just two to three simple lines.

To me, my home and its surroundings, taken together, are always the first place that roots me in this universe. To find and explore other such places, I travelled to places both near and far, crossing borders, seas, and shores. I found that I experienced them better on foot than by any other means.

2 KINDERGARTEN, THE GARDEN OF KIDS

Until I learnt German, I did not know that the meaning of Kindergarten is 'the garden of kids'. Gardens are adorned with various elements such as trees, plants, shrubs, flowers, fruits, pebbles, and water. A garden with a lot of flowers is a treat for our senses, offering flowers of different colours, sizes, shapes and textures, with or without nectar, scent or thorns; flowers that attract bees, beetles, butterflies or even tiny birds; flowers with varying budding and blooming hours, periods and seasons; flowers that are sacred, ornamental or medicinal; flowers that sprout onto stems, branches or creepers; and a lot more. Kids are also like flowers; not fully bloomed, but buds. Flowers in a garden appear to be aesthetically appealing when seen in a bunch or group. The artistic hands of a thoughtful gardener who gives them immense and unconditional love and care allow them to thrive. So is a Kindergarten; the kids being the flowers, and their mentors, the gardeners.

When I was a kid, I too was taken to such a garden, where my siblings finished their Kindergarten, in short KG. The fact that I can still remember the two years spent in my KG, from three decades ago illustrates how beautiful those visuals were. My first school was indeed a little paradise for me. It occupied elevated ground at the heart of my hometown, Nedumangad, located in the district of Thiruvananthapuram. The entrance arch facing the main road welcomed us with the name board of the school that read 'Darsana', a Sanskrit word with meanings like seeing, understanding, and philosophy.

From the arched gateway started an avenue-like pathway, both sides of which were lined with huge trees like *Gulmohar* (Delonix Regia), with their thick green foliage and red and yellow flowers. They made it almost impossible to see the school from outside and screened the views of and noise from the surrounding busy town. They gave shade to us and shelter to other beings. The pathway then transformed into a flight of about ten steps, leading us to the open court, around which the classrooms were arranged. Circulation spaces and open areas ran along the central axis of the school complex, dividing it into two parts. Buildings were juxtaposed around these common spaces, making the entire setting lively and safe.

There were altogether four buildings; one to the right side of the court was a tiled roof building which was painted light yellow; another to the left was an open-plan building which had a thatched roof, pillars, parapets and partition walls; the third one was beyond the former two, with a birds' cage at its entrance, which was the host venue for our class photos taken annually; and the fourth, sandwiched in between the first and the third, housed a playroom with equipment like rocking horse rides. All four buildings surrounded the open court, which was set on two levels with a height difference of less than a foot. The lower court separated the first two buildings, and the upper one separated the third and the fourth from the former two. The upper court, filled with sand, had play equipment including a see-saw and swings.

My first classroom in the Lower KG, 'LKG-A', was in the tiled-roof building, next to the Principal's room. The morning assemblies used to take place in the lower court, in front of our classroom. We had to climb a few steps to reach the classroom. It had a lot of small chairs in bright colours like red, blue, yellow, and green. The one-foot-high seat and the backrest of the chair were square-shaped. I still remember my classmates' faces then. Some were very silent, some were really naughty, some were screaming and weeping all the time, and others were simply enjoying sitting there. Any world, little or large, has to have variety for its existence, equilibrium and emergence!

During the first year of my KG, I could never travel on the school bus. Every morning, my father, who would be on his way to the office, would drop me off at school. Sometimes I reached there when the assembly was going on. In the evening, my mother would come and pick me up. I would walk ahead of her, and she would follow me with my school bag. Since it was a busy area, with a movie theatre, hospital, and a bus stand, we always kept to the pedestrian path. Around fifty metres away from my KG, there was a bakery from where my mother would buy me caramel chocolates and 5 Stars. Later on, it became a routine to buy chocolates on the way home. I used to run to the bakery, get chocolates from the bearded shopkeeper-uncle, and wait for my mother to come and pay for them.

My father always brought surprises for us when he came home from the office. Once he got me a set of pastel colours. With that, I painted a giraffe, brown and yellow ochre, in my favourite children's book '*Kalikkudukka*' (meaning magic pot). When the power went out, we lit a candle and sat around it on the floor. I continued painting, while my parents watched their little princess use colours to bring life to the lifeless drawing.

Various fun-filled activities filled my school days. Kids and parents crowded our school on the day Parle-G conducted a painting competition. After providing me with crayons and finding me a suitable place in the third building, my father went to wait outside with the other parents. I remember it as a noisy scene with so many people and their chatter, coupled with the tweets of the birds in the cage. Amidst the chaos, one teacher stepped in and delivered the instructions to be followed. She handed every kid a picture of a rabbit in a grassland. I was initially clueless about the colours to be chosen. Yet without a second thought, I coloured the rabbit yellow. While returning my artwork, I looked at my friends'. They were all different from mine, and most of them even painted it blue. “How come the same rabbit gets different colours!?” I wondered. In a few days, the result came, and I got third place. Wearing my new white frock, joined by my mother, siblings, and cousins, I went to school to receive my first-ever priceless prize. It was a bouquet of so many chocolates and biscuits, wrapped up in a shiny black cover, and a citation for the winner.

Running and the frog jump were my favourite sports at school. During a sports meet, thinking that I had reached the finishing point, I stopped somewhere in between. When I looked back, all others were far behind. My teachers encouraged me to jump forward, and so did I. When I reached the ‘real’ finishing point, they came running, hugged me tight, kissed me, and raised me high. For over two decades, my teachers pushed me forward, ensuring I never got stuck at virtual finishing points.

For the school’s annual day, my mother dressed me up like a traditional Muslim girl. Someone placed me at the centre of the stage. Seeing the crowd and feeling nervous in the new attire, I started crying. My tears wiped off the make-up on my face. Suddenly, seeing her student weeping, my class teacher came running and took me off the stage, as if she were removing a statue, for I had become entirely frozen.

As seasons changed, I got promoted to the next class, the Upper KG, 'UKG-E', and other changes followed. My classroom, this time, was in the thatched building, which had a single row of about five to six classes, divided by shared walls in between. I was becoming naughty by then. For effective control and surveillance, the teacher gave a light punishment to the naughtier ones by seating them in the first row to her left-hand side. Many a time, I had to sit beside the naughtiest one in the class. From our seats in the front row, we fought constantly over trifles such as pencils and sharpeners.

Another significant change was in my means of transportation to school. My parents stopped dropping me off at and picking me up from the KG. Instead, I was taken in the school bus that shuttled between my KG and the main campus of the same school, located a few kilometres apart. Mornings, the bus would collect everyone; the elder ones got off at their school, and the younger ones alighted at the KG. In the evenings, I would wait at the entrance steps for the bus from the main campus that brought senior students with it. The KG would then be left with only four to five kids, including me. Sometimes, to fight my boredom, I would pick up the fallen petals of the *Gulmohar* and make long red nails by attaching them to my tender nails. As soon as the bus arrived, my sister would peep through the glazed window in search of me—a sign of her protectiveness and presence. What I missed most on the bus journey was the walk with my mother along the pedestrian path, and my daily share of chocolates.

Kids who finished their Upper KG were transferred and upgraded to the main campus, provided they wanted to continue in the same school. Sadly, I had to leave my little paradise to join the new, bigger school, which was a 'jungle of buildings'. While studying in the dark, damp rooms of the ground floor reserved for new joiners, I realized just how much freshness and openness my first school had blessed us with. To my relief, I could visit my KG again, since I joined the music class, which used to take place there on most Sundays. However, it lasted only a few days. The Kindergarten stayed with its previous zeal for two more years until the main campus absorbed the KG section. And it remained deserted for a couple of years more.

When the town got a facelift in the name of 'development', new structures and uses like high-rise buildings, and hotels with bars mushroomed, making the surroundings even busier and unsafe for kids. The bakery from which I bought chocolates no longer exists. The Kindergarten has been erased from the town. Everything has been demolished and destroyed; my classrooms, playrooms, court, steps, the *Gulmohar*, birds' cage; the physicality of my school in its entirety was razed to the ground, leaving only its memories alive. Whenever I walk along that path, I look for traces of my school, even though I know I will not find any!

3 THE MUSEUM OF MY MEMOIRS

I do not remember the first time I visited the Museum and Zoo Complex in Thiruvananthapuram, as I have been there multiple times since I was a child. Being in an accessible location in the city, it formed one of our favourite destinations for recreation. My father would take us there whenever he got time and during almost every festive occasion.

While serving as a major landmark of the city, it has been drawing generations of visitors with its magnificence and majesty. It is called 'Museum' in an abridged version, even though it predominantly plays a dual role: that of a museum and of a zoo. The entrance to the complex is through two grand gateways, at both ends of its southern side, which abut the main road.

The pedestrian-friendly environs, coupled with the rich vegetation of its premises, make the Museum a favourite place for all age groups. The activities within the complex begin as early as morning with the routine maintenance work by staff, and the daily walks and exercises of joggers, who swarm in from places near and far. Every day feels vibrant in this one-stop destination bustling with people: solitude-seekers, couples seeking the shade of trees, families and groups of people picnicking or coming for a get together, school children from within and outside the state on excursions and study tours, college students coming from the institutions located nearby, and foreigners who tour through the city with the help of guides or otherwise. Besides being one of the germinating spots for ideas and public interest movements, the Museum has also been a favourite destination for generations of movie-makers. Joggers, who find the spot a favourite for maintaining their fitness, populate the complex in the evenings as well.

Other vibrant activities that occur mostly during weekends and on special and important days are painting competitions and art workshops. Most of them aim at creating social awareness or publicizing a new product or policy. Upon reaching upper primary, I began actively engaging in painting competitions held by various public and private organizations. A new world and a new family embraced me in the cityscape. I met many new kids there who later became my friends, colleagues, and students. Once, when I was taking part in a contest, a three-member family was curiously watching me from outside an enclosed garden within the complex. They were commenting on the way I was painting and how I was handling my paint tools with care; "See, now she wraps up her paintbrushes." My mother, who was standing beside them in the guise of a passerby, chuckled.

The history of the Museum complex is both interesting and informative. The Napier Museum was the first structure built in the complex in the mid-19th century. A zoo and a botanical garden were later added to that museum to attract more visitors. After about two decades, the original museum was demolished and reconstructed, and was named after the then Governor of Madras Presidency, Lord Francis Napier. The construction of other structures like the Natural History Museum, Sree Chithra Enclave, Sree Chitra Art Gallery, K.C.S. Paniker's Gallery, Reptile House, Auditorium, and other amenities followed as and when needs arose.

The Napier Museum, also called the Government Art Museum, is designed in the Indo-Saracenic architectural style, with a combination of Kerala, Mughal, Chinese, and Italian architecture. It houses exhibits of artistic, archeological, historic, and cultural importance, with collections like sculptures in metal and stone, carvings in wood and ivory, handicrafts like textiles and ornaments, traditional musical instruments, numismatic collections, and so on.

The Napier Museum sits on high ground, accessed from all four sides through steps. A long stretch of steps with a water fountain en route provides a grand entrance from the north. The porticos on the eastern and western ends, and the verandah to the south, act as seating spaces for people who seek its shade. The majestic walls and the sloping roof of the Napier Museum are visible from outside the complex, interspersed with the vegetation surrounding it.

The botanical garden has been integrated into the Museum premises and the zoo, rather than letting it be a standalone entity. It includes trees, shrubs, ornamental plants, hedges, creepers, etc. The entire complex, spreading over around 22 hectares, acts as the lung of the city. During the day, people can be seen resting beneath the trees or lounging on the lawns.

The gigantic banyan tree (*Ficus benghalensis*), the foliage of which spanned several metres, giving shade to the Napier Museum to the north and to the lawns on all other sides, got uprooted due to ageing and climatic reasons. It left a void not only in the complex but also in the memories of all who loved its shade, the rustle of its leaves, and the abundance of fresh air it provided, and even the mere presence and sight of it. To me, it was like the 'mother of all trees' in the complex. The raised platform built around the banyan tree was the location I was really fond of. The space around the tree, adorned with other trees like *champak* (Magnolia champaca) and *Asoka* (Saraca asoca), was the open-air venue for most of the painting competitions wherein I had taken part. After the creative work, I would play with my friends underneath the banyan tree for hours. We even shared meals under the smaller trees, which were sheltered by the banyan's vast canopy.

The lawns beside the banyan tree hosted my first ever painting exhibition with twenty-four other friends of mine, on the occasion of *Vishu* (a harvest festival of Kerala). At that time, I met an old couple from Westminster, London, and gifted them one of my paintings that wasn't on display. They were delighted and asked me to write my contact details on the back of the painting. A month later, a letter from the United Kingdom arrived at my house. "See this!" I rushed to my mother. It was a letter sent by the same couple, with a photo of themselves standing in front of the framed picture I had gifted them. They were ardent travellers who spent their vacations touring different places. And when both of them retired, they got enough time to roam around together. They used to send me letters and postcards from wherever they went afterwards, sometimes a detailed note of those visits.

The zoo, being another major focus area in the complex, is located further north of the Napier Museum. Providing habitat for many indigenous and exotic species, the zoo conserves the faunal and floral wealth, apart from providing recreation to the visitors. Although the zoo and the botanical garden were established to attract more visitors, they have also been serving the purpose of ex-situ conservation. A residential zone neighbours the northern boundary of the zoo, and every day those residents can watch animals housed at the northern fringe of the zoo, such as elephants, giraffes, and deer. Roads border the eastern and western sides, but thick vegetation buffers them.

My parents still recount their visits to the zoo with my brother when he was a little child. He used to narrate the details of those visits to his grandfather, like the variety and number of animals and birds, their gestures and sounds, the way hippopotamuses (which he mistook as another kind of elephant) spouted water, half immersed in the pool.

Animals differ in their territorial needs, as do the sizes of the enclosures provided to them. Some, like lions, bears, and monkeys, get a bigger, open-to-sky, enclosed habitat. Ferocious ones, including lions, tigers, and leopards, are kept in cages with different compartments. Those in groups or large numbers, such as deer and zebra, are kept inside fences. Some, like elephants, giraffes, and rhinos, get a vast area to roam around. The area where birds are kept, especially the one with water birds, is often the noisiest of all in the zoo, because of their chirps, tweets, and shrieks.

The city would remain on alert when inmates escaped from the zoo. A missing gray langur was in the breaking news for two days, during which time it was spotted, caught, and brought back to the zoo. Having just been transferred with its partner and completing a week-long quarantine, the langur escaped the zoo during a trial release into its enclosure. Though given utmost care and attention, sometimes I feel sorry for the inmates, as they will live as exhibits, kept inside green coloured bars and cages, for the visual pleasure of humans who would otherwise have to visit them in their natural habitats scattered in different geographies. Seeing the happiness and astonishment of kids and first-timers, I also realized its educational purpose.

During my second winter vacation in New Delhi, where I was doing my Master's, I paid a solo visit to the zoo in Thiruvananthapuram. Those days, I was doing my field visits for my thesis, travelling around thirty kilometres all the way from my home to the project site in the morning, and traversing the same distance back home in the evening. On one such day, to get rid of the monotony in commuting, I stopped by the Museum and strolled in the zoo. It was undeniably a refreshing day for me as I enjoyed every moment of it. I did not even bother to click a single photo with my camera.

On every visit, the zoo had something new to offer. And on that day too, I had a feeling that I was visiting it for the first time. It had been over ten years since I last saw the zoo, though I did occasionally visit the Napier Museum and its surroundings. The zoo had changed a lot. There were many more species of animals and birds, all kept in spacious and well-maintained quarters that suited each one. Some of the enclosures had been modified with artificial caves, water bodies, and improved landscaping features. Some animals had been moved to new enclosures. The zoo's layout, including the entrance and exit, had been redesigned. I remember seeing porcupines and foxes at the end of the trail during my childhood. But this time, peacocks and reptiles occupied the areas near the exit gates. For a very long period, the reptiles had been kept in a dedicated building, called the Reptile House, to the east of the Napier Museum. It was under maintenance and was about to be converted into an aquarium. The reptiles were relocated to a new home near the exit gate of the zoo.

The Children's Park is an exclusive entertainment area at the Museum, because the other spots offer educational value as well. I fondly remember spending many evenings playing there with my siblings. It had a variety of rides, such as a merry-go-round, swings, and slides. As we were regulars, it felt like our own neighbourhood park. Exhausted after all the fun at the park, we always had ice cream or apple juice from the KTDC's (Kerala Tourism Development Corporation) parlour, or coffee and snacks from the restaurant next to it.

The Museum is also a destination for art enthusiasts. The Sree Chitra Art Gallery houses the collections of Shri Chithira Tirunal (the last ruling Maharaja of Travancore): paintings of Raja Ravi Varma, Nicholas Roerich and contemporary painters; works of schools of art with origins in India and abroad; miniatures; and manuscripts. Art and aesthetics are found outside the galleries as well. During one visit, while we were looking at the artwork, it began to pour, and the branches of the trees swayed in the wind that blew with the rain. When the weather cleared, we came out, only to find the entrance path of the Gallery carpeted in '*Manchadi*' (red lucky seeds), that had fallen from the tree in its forecourt. I joined my sister in picking up those small, vermillion seeds shed by the tree in the heavy rain and wind. We treasured them in a transparent glass jar.

The K.C.S. Paniker's Gallery, located behind the Aquarium (formerly the Reptile House), features contemporary Indian art by the artist himself. An auditorium occupies the upper storey of the same building, where seminars, lecture series, or exhibitions are often organized. The second exhibition of my paintings was held in this auditorium, conducted in memory of a dedicated photographer who lost his life capturing a landslide in the district. I have been to the auditorium as an invitee as well.

Another major landmark in the complex is the bandstand (or band-station), located immediately east of the Napier Museum. It is a pavilion-like structure characterized by a high stone plinth, wooden railings, stone pillars, and a sloping roof. People can listen to the evening broadcast played on the radio mounted upon it. The bandstand is encircled by an open circular court, with park benches positioned along the outer edge. The court is accessed from different sides through archways and pathways lined by neatly pruned shrubs and flowering plants, including bougainvillea. Special programmes are arranged at the bandstand during festive occasions. As a child, I watched in awe as martial arts were performed on its premises during *Onam*, the official state festival of Kerala.

With family, my experience of the Museum was confined to specific areas, like the zoo, park, and botanical garden, owing to our activities being primarily for entertainment. Other services offered at the Museum complex gradually unfolded to me over time. During a high school field trip, we visited the Natural History Museum inside the complex. What fascinated me the most was the jawbone of a whale, which was longer than I imagined it to be! Taxidermy of animals and birds (the art of preserving skins for a realistic look), displayed with natural expressions, and ethnographic models of traditional houses are just a few of the many attractions found there.

Same place, different roles to play at different times. For kids, the Museum is their park, their zoo, and indisputably a school that teaches them more than a classroom can. Solo travellers find it a place for their self-discovery. Couples see it as an Eden. Students who take a break from college find it a perfect hangout. Families view it as a 'one-size-fits-all' destination. Researchers treasure it as an invaluable repository of knowledge.

The long years of association with the Museum and zoo complex have made it feel like a second home for me. There, I had spent a major part of my life with my family and friends. I have been familiar with every square inch of it and have seen the many transformations it has undergone. My parents still go there with their grandchildren, with the same enthusiasm and energy they had when they took their first child to the zoo.

The Museum complex continues to be busy with the hustle and bustle of people, the rustle of leaves, and the chirping of birds. I wish it would remain there with its inherent vitality for many more generations to come; to entertain, educate, and provide a sense of well-being to all. Whenever I plan a get-together with my friends or colleagues, I invariably ask them, "Can we meet at the Museum?"

4 OUR CHILDHOOD SANDBOX

Childhood memories remain fresh in my mind, as they do for most of us. The best of those were spent with my parents and siblings. Every weekend or on off days, my father would take all of us to our favourite places in the city of Thiruvananthapuram: parks, museums, beaches, and so on. As part of our outings, we used to go to Shankhumukham beach almost every month. *Shankhu* means conch, and *mukham* means face.

Shankhumukham beach is accessed by road, en route to the domestic airport in the city. The seashore is flanked by the Laccadive Sea (Lakshadweep Sea) region of the Arabian Sea to the west. The beach, children's park, Old Indian Coffee House (ICH), *Arattumandapam* (a pillared hall), and an enormous sculpture of a mermaid (called *Sagarakanyaka* or *Jalakanyaka*) are still some of the major attractions there.

Upon reaching the beach, we would have a quick glimpse of the sea. All of us would then proceed to the children's park, which resembled a grove of trees. We were regular users of the park and its amenities. Collecting three tickets, my siblings would fetch their bicycles. Being young, I was supposed to stay with my parents. They would bring me a tricycle, walk with me, and guide me as I rode along the paths. Growing up, I could join my siblings, but the bicycle my parents chose for me had training wheels. Kids of various age groups could be seen riding bicycles carefully through the tracks, following the traffic rules stipulated in the park. There were well-laid-out tracks, traffic signals, and bicycle bays to teach the kids about traffic rules and the need to follow them strictly from a very young age. Once we had finished cycling, we would park the bicycles in the parking lot.

Leaving the park, we might spend some time near the *Sagarakanyaka* or *Jalakanyaka* (sculpture of a mermaid) by the renowned sculptor Kanayi Kunhiraman. From there, we would move toward the beach, which by then would be bustling with families, children, and couples. The arrival of the crowd cheered up another set of people—the vendors selling pinwheels, balloons, toys, cotton candy, *soan papdi*, sweets, fried peanuts; solo or group performers engaged in songs, street circuses, and other shows; owners who brought their ponies and horses for rides along the beach. Kites of many colours, patterns, finishes, and textures were a true delight for the eyes. The sand, the sea, and the sky would all be busy entertaining the crowd that kept pouring onto the beach.

After letting me dip my feet in the waves that travelled all the way from the deep sea to the shore, my parents would take me back. As there had been a previous mishap involving the sea, I was supposed to stay as far from the seashore as I could. I was miraculously saved on Mahabalipuram beach from the waves that had tried to grab me from my parents twice. My brother and sister, being older, could play with the waves as long as they wished. They used to laugh at me and make fun of me, as being the youngest, I did not have the liberties that they had enjoyed then. To join their team was one reason I wanted to grow up fast. The beach was versatile, and had many roles to play for us: it became a playground when we wanted to run on it; became clay when we sculpted our home, castle, trenches and reliefs of various sorts; and became our writing board when we engraved our names on it only to be washed away by the incoming and outgoing waves. It was by all means, a bigger sandbox for us.

When we were done playing in the waves and the sand, we would have our refreshments at the Indian Coffee House across the beach road. It is an imposing structure with a steep-sloped roof and high walls embellished with pilasters. The arched windows and doors, and the rectangular ventilator windows above them, give the façade a distinct character. It sits on a platform accessed by stairs and enclosed by a perforated parapet. The open, terrace-like dining space faces the beach. We would find a table for ourselves in the shade of the overhang and have our coffee and snacks, enjoying the sea breeze and the views around.

Returning to the sandy area on the beach, we used to watch the sun slowly diving into the sea. Even at night, people would crowd onto the beach, and allied businesses would thrive as usual.

Besides serving the mentioned activities, the beach has also been a major venue for many events. To name a few, it hosts political events including conferences, protests and rallies; stage shows or performances of music and dance; promotions of any movement or events for a social cause; art competitions and athletic meets; and religious rituals like the immersion of Lord *Ganesha*'s idols during *Vinayaka Chaturthi* (the birthday of Lord *Ganesha*), and *bali tharpanam* (the rituals done for the dead by their beloved). *Shankhumukham* also has ties with the erstwhile kingdom of Travancore. It has been the '*Aarattukadavu*' (the bank for ceremonial bath) of the presiding deity (Lord *Anantha*) of the Sri Padmanabhaswamy Temple, in the city of Thiruvananthapuram (thiru-anantha-puram meaning the city of Lord Anantha). The procession of *Aarattu* to the beach is led by the incumbent Maharaja of Travancore, who holds the royal sword in hand. I have seen most of this happen on this same versatile beach that has also been the backdrop for many joyful moments with my loved ones.

Over the years, as the number of people flocking to the beach increased and their needs expanded, new additions sprouted—including art museums, abstract sculptures of relaxing people, parks near the Jalakanyaka, a Traffic Training Park, a destination wedding venue, and open-air exhibits of the air force.

While travelling to the airport along the beach road, I would search for my favourite spots in Shankhumukham. In each such journey, I tried to cherish my childhood memories, which were still cradled by the waves with care and affection. I understood that the law of nature leaves no stone unturned; it applies to this beach as well. The bicycle park is no longer in operation, and the site has lost its old charm. The Indian Coffee House, once on the verge of demolition, was rescued by an outcry from heritage enthusiasts and the nostalgic public.

Coastal erosion led to the gradual shrinking of the beach, which was more than a hundred metres in width. The Laccadive Sea ate away most of the beach road that runs parallel to the seashore. Embankments built to protect the beach and road from further erosion failed to fight the might of the sea, hungry for the shore. Instead of the fine sand on the beach, now boulders and granite of various sizes line the shore. The gradual slope of the beach is replaced by the abrupt cut caused by the reinforcement of the embankment. To reach the airport, one can now bypass the old beach road by entering the one near the mermaid sculpture, suggesting the inevitable erosion that threatens the rest of the shoreline. At times, the beach road was closed due to violent sea erosion, and the beach itself was closed to the public for a few years, only to be reopened partially. Beautification projects, redevelopment projects, and shore management plans are being implemented on the beach to restore its old glory as a major cultural space in the city.

In fact, the sea eroded the setting of the memories of many. The deep-diving sun has been the prime witness to all the ups and downs of the beach, and the sole listener of its sorrows. I hope the tears of the beach will be washed away by the incoming waves and dissolved in the salty sea.

The 'conch-faced' beach—its mermaid, sand, waves, the children's park, bicycles, cotton candies, pinwheels, the Coffee House—all of it would remain as indelible episodes of my childhood, whether or not the sea encroaches again or the beach shrinks further. I am sure that the cycle of erosion can only apply to material things; it can in no way stop the process of memory building.

5 FROM THE NATIONAL BAL BHAVAN TO THE RASHTRAPATI BHAVAN

On that winter night in November 2005, as I took my first step into the National Bal Bhavan on Kotla Road, New Delhi, I did not have a hint of what was in store for me. The National Level Selection Camp for the National Bal Shree Honour was set to begin the next day, bringing together students from different states who had successfully completed the regional (District) and zonal (State) levels. My stream was Creative Arts, and I was part of a five-member contingent, escorted by two staff members, from Thiruvananthapuram.

We landed in Delhi after a three-day-long train journey, and some of us struggled against the odds, including a bout of food poisoning. I was new to Delhi and curious to see what this metro city would offer. Because of the heavy and intermittent traffic, we reached Bal Bhavan late at night. As the night was so chilly, everyone went to sleep right away in the huge dormitory allotted to us. While everyone fell asleep, I was awake until midnight, thinking of my hopes and wishes regarding the camp. Meanwhile, a girl with short hair entered our dormitory with her mother and took the vacant bed next to mine. Seeing me awake, she broke the ice by introducing herself as Akanksha, another contestant in

Creative Arts. We talked for a few minutes until the air became frigid, making it impossible to prolong the conversation.

The next day, I woke up early and took a bath in icy cold water. It was a test I had put myself through: a test of my determination and courage. I became the 'superwoman' in front of myself and those who had warned me to stay away from cold water during winter. After having breakfast at the canteen, we moved to the Sports Centre, where everyone was supposed to gather to attend the first session of the camp. It was planned to make us stress-free and performance-ready for the forthcoming week. The objective was to bring out the finest form of creativity among the participating children, which necessitated a truly unique selection process.

The National Bal Shree Honour was instituted by the National Bal Bhavan (NBB) to identify and enhance the creative potential of children in four streams: Performance, Arts, Writing, and Scientific Innovation. The NBB is a brainchild of India's first Prime Minister, Pandit Jawaharlal Nehru, whom children fondly called '*Chacha*' (meaning uncle). He conceived it in 1956 as an institution for non-formal learning, complementary to the formal education system, to develop the creativity and potential in all children by providing equitable opportunities.

The NBB functions as the apex body of the State Bal Bhavans. In addition, the establishment of Bal Bhavans in rural areas ensures the inclusion of children from areas hitherto untouched by and outside the zone of influence of the State Bal Bhavans, which are mostly located in urban centres. The environs of the Bal Bhavan and its activities echo the noble idea of enriching the creative potential of India's childhood. The NBB campus has been designed for children to learn, play, and interact creatively with their surroundings, contributing to their individual development and helping shape them into better human beings.

After walking the grounds several times over the following days, I made a blueprint of the premises of NBB in my mind. Going past the security outpost at the entrance gate, one can find birds kept in large cages. Proceeding further, a huge ground welcomes us, around which all the buildings on the campus are sited. To the east, beyond the birds' cage, lies a village-like setting, featuring huts painted with Warli art, models of bullocks and a well. During the camp, my team painted a theme on the side of the compound wall that faces the ground. To the east of the ground lies the National Children's Museum and the Mekhala Jha Auditorium, where performances and lectures used to take place. The venue for Creative Arts was in a building further north of the Mekhala Jha Auditorium. Staff quarters and a hostel with dormitories and a canteen are to the north of the ground. Administrative blocks and dedicated classrooms for music, musical instruments, painting, etc., are to the west, next to the amphitheatre that hosts cultural events and screens movies. The Sports Centre is in the northwest corner of the ground.

The camp gave me the finest opportunity to see so many young, talented faces of different age groups from different parts of India. A similar enthusiasm shone on everyone else's faces. Together, we handled the tough competition with ease, and in all the sessions, we put forth our best creative ideas. During off-timings, we gathered at the ground, sat in circles, and had our discussions, fun sessions, and games. I also made many good friends. A week flew by in the blink of an eye, and just like that, the camp was over. In low spirits, everyone parted ways with the NBB, not knowing if we would ever see each other again.

Even after reaching home, the NBB and Delhi were always in my thoughts and dreams. I was reluctant to return to school, as I had been on a two-week leave to attend the national camp. During breaks, I used to share accounts of my 'Delhi days' with my friends, who were excited to listen to the same. One day, to my surprise, I received a letter from Sharmila from Tamil Nadu, who was a co-participant in Creative Arts. I was delighted to see her letter, and a photo of us sitting on the ground of the NBB with other friends. I am a person who cherishes souvenirs like these, be it a photo, a letter, or a gift. Quality friendships that last a lifetime always keep me motivated to make new friends.

Days passed, and good tidings came from Delhi, confirming my inclusion on the final list. The news came when I was attending the annual school day function. It was a proud moment when my school's Principal announced the result, describing my achievement as a feather in the cap of the school. I did not have a hint about another surprise that was awaiting me. On the first working day following the annual school day, I reached school earlier than my usual time. On seeing me, my classmates asked why I hadn't come later that day. Although I wondered at their query, I found them busy with some preparations. Finally, the surprise was revealed in the first hour itself when they requested our class teacher to provide a few minutes to conduct a felicitation function. The entire class applauded me for the accomplishment, and our teacher gifted me the 'citation', 'memento' and 'bouquet'. The 'citation' was a lovely handwritten letter of appreciation, the 'memento' was a cute little pyramidal tower that lights up when it is on, and the 'bouquet' was an artificial rose flower. I still treasure them among my favourite souvenirs, and the 'memento' is kept near the memento I had received from the President at a later date.

The official invitation from the NBB came home inviting me to receive the prestigious National Bal Shree Honour 2005, from the President of India, at the Rashtrapati Bhavan in New Delhi. In May 2006, during the summer vacation after my ninth standard exam, I caught the train to Delhi again, this time with my parents and sister. Knowing the purpose behind our trip, the co-passengers in our bogie, who had been strangers until then, became like family.

After we had covered about half the distance, news of people fainting and dying under the scorching sun in the North made us worried about the climate we would be exposed to in a few hours. Having been acquainted with the tropical monsoon climate in Kerala, we were bothered by the climatic variability. As the distance to Delhi was decreasing, we could feel the mercury rising. I still cannot forget the wave of intense heat and dust that greeted us at the railway station in Delhi. During the sizzling summer, Delhi looked completely dry, exposing the other extreme of its climate, about six months after my last visit. I realized the severity of the summers, which were far more grueling than the winters.

We checked in at the Kerala House on Jantar Mantar Road. As the winners had to stay at the NBB itself, I unpacked everything and packed my bag separately. The next morning, we arrived at the NBB, and I was so thrilled to see my friends again, especially Akanksha. While I was spending time with my friends and my father was talking with their parents, my mother and sister chose to explore the campus instead, which I had already outlined for them. That was when a lady asked them something in Hindi. They hardly knew Hindi in its colloquial form, though both of them were familiar with the formal language from school. They replied to her in broken Hindi, "*Hindi nahi maloom*", quoting a line from a *Malayalam* movie. Hearing them, the lady continued to ask questions. Growing weary of repeating themselves, they fled the scene. After having lunch, my family went back, and I stayed at the NBB hostel.

A week prior to the award ceremony, a lot of preparatory sessions took place at the NBB: the making of the painting which was to be gifted to the President, the practice of the performances to be staged, the many rounds of flawless rehearsal sessions for receiving the award, the purchase of Kolhapuri chappals from Janpath, and the opening of *Kisan Vikas Patra* (which was part of the award) at the Post Office nearby.

A grand party was arranged for the winners at the NBB campus on the eve of the award function. We had to wear the extra dress provided by NBB, which was to be worn for the award ceremony. After lunch, everyone hurried to iron their clothes, as the party was to commence in a few hours. I went to the dormitory to get mine, kept in my bag near my bed. Unfortunately, my dress went missing, and I trembled. Worried about what to do next, I desperately ran out of the hostel. And I spotted Eshani's mother coming towards the hostel, with her daughter's dress ironed. Before I could ask her anything, she affectionately handed over my dress, which was so neatly pressed. She was staying with Eshani in the same dormitory as mine. While taking her daughter's dress for ironing, she thought of getting mine ironed too. My eyes filled with tears of joy as I thanked her for her kind gesture. She just smiled, as she always used to.

In the evening, the lawn at the NBB was brilliantly illuminated. It was converted into a grand party area, with chairs dressed in white satin cloth, and buffet counters arranged under various pavilions. It was an evening filled with smiles and sparkles—of the winners, their parents and relatives, staff at the NBB, and the special guests and invitees. At the party, we unveiled the painting to be gifted to the President. The day concluded with a scrumptious dinner and a photo session, and the dreams of many creative minds.

Putting an end to the week-long preparations, the much-awaited day of 15th May 2006 arrived. All twenty-two winners of the Award, from four distinct streams, had been longing for that very moment. By noon, everyone got dressed up in white-coloured *kurta*s and pants, beige-coloured Nehru jackets, and *Kolhapuri* chappals, except for the dancers who wore their traditional dance costumes for the performances to be staged in the venue. Every face was filled with joy and pride, knowing very well that it was a milestone in our creative careers. As we were travelling to the venue in a van, I told Akanksha, "My dream is about to come true!" She nodded as if she also had the same dream.

We finally reached the venue, the Rashtrapati Bhavan, the office and the official residence of the President of India, on Raisina Hill in New Delhi. Its construction was completed in 1929, after the British had shifted India's capital from Calcutta to Delhi in 1911. The historically significant structure was the imperial residence of the Viceroy of India during British rule in India. It is a monumental building, crafted by a British architect named Edwin Lutyens and inspired by Indian architecture. Over 300 rooms of varying sizes and purposes are housed in this four-storeyed structure. Built with brick and stone, it is faced with pink sandstone and cream Dholpur stone, featuring a black dome on top, high plinths, pillars, *chhajja*s, *chhatri*s, *jali*s, and motifs, among others. I was overwhelmed by the history, art, and architecture of this monumental edifice that occupies an elevated position at the heart of India's seat of power.

We passed through many security checks, and during one, I was asked to remove something from my jacket pocket. When I told them I wanted to take it inside, they agreed because it was harmless. Everybody took their respective seats in the hall that was arranged for the award ceremony. The front two rows were for the winners, and the rear ones were reserved for the 'real winners', the proud parents. My sister could not attend the ceremony, and I still feel sad that my siblings could not witness their youngest sister receiving the award. It is a reward that I believe is the result of a combined effort made by my family, extending their invaluable blessings, love, patience, prayers, and sacrifices. All our beloved mentors and staff from the NBB had reached the hall by that time, and they were coordinating everything. They reminded each one of us to perform our roles as planned, and if possible, better. Everyone's body language was filled with confidence and pride.

A few moments later, they informed us that we should be ready. Thereafter, a pin-drop silence fell over the hall. We understood that the most awaited moment had come. Someone entered the hall at a fast pace, who was none other than Dr A.P.J. Abdul Kalam! The function began officially, and the dignitaries on the dais delivered their speeches. In his motivating speech, the President advised us to become good human beings, and we all took an oath together.

It was time to honour the winners, who, upon the announcement of their names, would go and stand on a carpet to the left of the dais. Our parents' names were also called, upon which they would rise from their seats. The awardees would wait there until the reading of their citation was completed. The citation is unique and custom-made for each winner, as it mentions their family, their talents, and their performance in the selection process. Once it is complete, they head towards the dais. The ninth was my turn. I moved to the red carpet, my parents rose from their seats, and the description followed: "Miss. Jessin Kabir……." I held my head high, feeling proud and happy that my talent got recognized at a prestigious event. Once it was over, I walked towards him, and he handed over the citation and the memento to me, an honour which every kid would long to bag. He smiled at me and congratulated me. I was on cloud nine! It was such a glorious moment! I went back to my seat, as if I were still dreaming about it.

Omkar from Creative Writing was in his wheelchair, and his mother was directing him towards the dais. This sight softened the heart of the 'Missile Man', who came down from the dais and honoured him—an unexpected and acclaimed gesture from the first citizen of India! Subsequently, tremendous applause filled the hall. We, the crew of Creative Arts, presented him with the painting that we had made, which highly impressed him. He was particularly pleased that some of the unique ideas behind it were contributed by Omkar. The dance and musical performances made it a truly divine ceremony, which was brought to a close with the National Anthem.

Following the award function, we were all set for a photo session. While everyone rose from their seats and searched for ideal locations to pose, I approached him and informed him that I was from Kerala. He greeted me with his innocent smile, which reminded me of the hidden object in my pocket. It was my autograph book! I took it out and extended it to him. He wrote on a page, "Greeting", with his signature below. Nothing seemed more exciting to me at that moment than getting the autograph of a much-respected and beloved President! The photo session began, and I took a place right next to him. Having spent a little more time with us, he left the hall. Soon, everyone vacated the hall, had tea arranged for us, and left for the NBB.

I always relish and cherish happy endings. That day not only had a happy ending, but was also full of happiness throughout. "Was it all a dream?!" I wondered.

Reaching the NBB, I packed my bag to join my family, who had been touring Delhi for the past week. When we were about to leave for the Kerala House, I saw Akanksha crying at the gate. We tried to console her, but in vain. Until the NBB gate faded from view, we could still spot her at the gate. It was a scene that none of us could ever forget. Time and distance could separate us, but our bonds remained strong through letters and phone calls.

The next day, we got calls from people we knew and also from the press. My photo of receiving the award from the President appeared in newspapers. Many pointed out that the highlight of the photo was our nearly identical smiles. "Wasn't it the same? Of course, it was!" I was convinced, as others were, after seeing the New Delhi edition of a regional newspaper which featured the same photograph.

That day, we were travelling to Agra in a tourist bus. Time and again, the weather disappointed us by acting like an oven, baking us in high temperatures. Wherever we had to remove our shoes, we were literally hopping, instead of walking, across the scorching pathways and floors around the monuments. Even with my half-closed eyes, I could not properly enjoy the beauty of that world wonder, the Taj Mahal. The impressive Agra Fort, Akbar's Tomb, and Mathura were the other destinations that we covered that day. On returning to Kerala House, I packed the souvenirs we had bought from Agra, including the marble miniature of the Taj Mahal, as we were leaving Delhi in two days' time.

Those days, Kerala House was abuzz with politicians and press people, as it was an eventful week back in Kerala too, where the results of the Legislative Assembly election had just been declared. Leaders and prominent figures soon flew to Delhi. My family met Shri. V.S. Achuthanandan, who won the Assembly elections and was to be sworn in as the next Chief Minister of Kerala. I could not meet him, as I was at the NBB. The former Chief Minister of Kerala, Shri. A.K. Antony was staying on our floor. We went to meet him, and on knowing about the award, he congratulated me and gave me chocolates.

On our second-to-last day in Delhi, we spent a whole day with the Jacobs, our family friends. The return trip was particularly exciting because it was our first time on the Delhi Metro. I understood how a mass rapid transit system could ease travelling in a metro city, bypassing the busy and blocked roads and neighbourhoods, teeming with heavy traffic and crowds.

That evening, we went to meet my father's friend, the late

Shri. D. Vijayamohan, who was a journalist, writer, and editor working in Delhi. The network of roads and roundabouts seemed identical to us, and it was confusing. On the way to his office, the auto-driver himself got confused with the roads; I think we saw the same roundabout at least five times that evening. At some point, we even thought that he might be misleading us. Newcomers may experience a lack of orientation, finding themselves hopelessly lost unless they have a map or can navigate using landmarks and other methods.

The same wave of intense heat and dust that had welcomed us in Delhi bid us farewell upon leaving. Conversely, what welcomed us in Kerala was pleasant weather, as the Southwest monsoon was at the doorstep. What I found unpleasant was the start of tenth-grade classes, now that summer vacation was over. But the year had more surprises in store for me. The first chapter in our Hindi textbook featured a segment from Dr A.P.J. Abdul Kalam's autobiography, *Wings of Fire*. Every time I used to read that chapter, I wished that the first page featured his autograph! It would remain as a wish only—I know! His autobiography is a testimony to the simple, yet great and inspiring life he lived. Even in his absence, he continues to ignite young minds.

A year later, after I joined my new school, I was called back to Delhi. The NBB organized an alumni meet of the Bal Shree awardees on 14th November 2007, Children's Day. I was the only Bal Shree awardee on the team, which comprised five students and two staff members from the State Bal Bhavan, Thiruvananthapuram. The faculty member who escorted us was Sreekumar Sir, a specialist in the tabla. He used to sing songs and explain their various aspects and nuances methodically. It was from him that I leant the fundamentals of musical beats, how to keep count, and the concept of different ragas. The students on our team were also learning music at the Bal Bhavan. They sang songs with their teacher, and as everyone shared their knowledge of music, the monotonous train journey turned into a musical one. During the selection camp, the *Mridangam* teacher at the Bal Bhavan, Suresh Sir, was the one who had come with us. The association with these two mentors induced in me an affinity for music.

We reached NBB in the evening, and it was only mildly cold outside. Seeing me, Akanksha came running and hugged me. In the days that followed, I spotted other co-recipients as well. That was a week well spent with some old and new friends.

At the camp, I met the young writer and Bal Shree awardee, Dr Niyati, who was then pursuing her undergraduate studies at Delhi University. We used to talk about a lot of things—her dreams and aspirations, her life in Delhi, her writing journey, and the beauty of Malayalam vocabulary—all of which gave me a lot of valuable insights. From her accounts, I came to know a little more about the non-resident Keralites in Delhi, the temple at Mayur Vihar, the local cuisine in Delhi, and more.

Many activities were planned for the alumni meet: cultural events, musical performances, and art workshops. The Creative Arts alumni painted a mural on the wall overlooking the ground. The musical performances by the team led by Neha Sharma—a singer and senior Bal Shree Awardee—fascinated everyone.

Towards the end of the camp, we went out for purchases. On every visit to the NBB, I used to go shopping at the many lively markets in Delhi: Janpath, Palika Bazar, Sarojini Nagar, Lajpath, Karol Bagh, etc. Numerous monuments and edifices dot Delhi's cityscape, echoing the architectural and artistic marvels of a bygone era. I really loved the warmth that early winter offers. Dr Niyati's accounts, coupled with my own experience, instilled a new dream in my mind: to study in Delhi.

I came back home, feeling contented to have seen Delhi, the NBB, and my dear friends thrice, over three consecutive years; twice in winter and once in summer. During the All India Tour in my undergraduate studies, in 2013, we halted for a day at the Travancore House on Kasturba Gandhi Marg in New Delhi. We had a flavoursome dinner at our classmate's home nearby.

Six and a half years later, I reached Delhi to live there for two years for my Masters in Architectural Conservation at the School of Planning and Architecture (SPA) Delhi. After my first semester exam, I thought of visiting the NBB before going home for the winter vacation. The gravity of winter was increasing day by day, and so reaching the hostel before it got too cold at night was of utmost importance. I went with my classmate Gopika, who was also a Bal Shree Awardee. We trudged through the busy roads and finally located the NBB on Kotla Road, which was within walking distance of our college. It is a strange irony that sometimes we fail to notice our dearest things, not knowing their close proximity to us.

On entering the campus, I thought of my first winter night at the NBB, nine years ago. We sat on the long steps facing the ground, reliving our memories there, though separate in time. Then I took a quick look at all my favourite spots on campus. While walking along the corridor of the classroom block, I heard a song sung in a very husky and sweet voice. Somebody was singing with a harmonium in one of the classrooms. Both the teacher and the students were sitting on a carpeted floor. I entered the room and was surprised to find that the voice belonged to Neha Sharma, who was teaching music to her students! We exchanged smiles and words. I wondered, "Such a small world!"

6 A NEW COLOUR FOR KANNUR

'A Festival Procession' was the topic for the watercolour competition in the District Youth Festival at High School. I began applying colour to the pencil outlines on the drawing sheet provided. *Theyyam*, *Velichappadu* (oracle), *Kathakali*, etc., were the central characters in the theme of an Onam procession ideated by me. I usually stop working on anything whenever my mind says "Finished!" That day, I reached my finishing point much before the time limit given to us. I won and got the chance to take part in the State Youth Festival to be held at Kannur in 2007.

Colours form one attribute that helps me recognize and associate the tangibles and intangibles that I come across in life, say, the days of a week, seasons, places, people, and incidents. And the colour changes when my perceptions about those things change. To me, Kannur was the land of the leftists, of protests and violence, of human beings with strong willpower, of the powerful divine characters in the folk and traditional arts like *Theyyam*, and so on. Thus, I assigned Kannur the colour red; the redness of fire and blood, of aggressiveness, anger, caution, danger, determination, desire, energy, passion, power, revenge, radiance and vibrance.

We arrived in Kannur two days before the competition. All

arrangements were already in place for our stay at the Government Guest House by the sea. Of all the districts in Kerala, Kannur has the longest seashore. The one major advantage of the room allotted to us was that it had a balcony that faced the Arabian Sea, which was hardly fifty metres away. I liked that room as I had always dreamt of having a home facing the sea. Waves of varying sizes and strengths smashed against the heap of angular, jet-black rocks lining the coastline. The waves struck the rocks, splashing the water partly onto the shore and partly onto the sea. During our stay there, I loved spending time on the balcony, and I kept on giving commentary to myself about the 'wave show' at the land-sea transition zone; "Yes! This one will hit the boulder with its full strength! Ah! Great! There you are!"

While we were having dinner in the guest house's restaurant, four foreigners occupied the table diagonally to our left. One of the two women had her hair styled in sections; her ears, eyebrows, and chin were pierced with silver ornaments, her wrists were stacked with bangles, and tattoos were scattered across her arms. The other three shared a similar aesthetic, and they seemed entirely unconcerned with how others might judge their appearance. We shared smiles.

The sea was quite restless, even at night, and our room seemed like a floating lagoon in the deep blue sea. In the morning, the cool breeze from the sea, which was so rejuvenating, woke me up.

The next day, taking my painting tools, we set out for the Youth Festival venue at the core of the city. The tiled-roof school building, which had hosted the competition, helped block the sun to a great extent. The topic suited the situation we were in: 'Man's atrocities against Mother Earth'. Global temperature rise is the byproduct of man's ignorance of and utter disregard for his 'homeland'. It is not Earth's revenge against man, but rather her natural response to the stimuli introduced by man. If we cut trees, there is no escape route other than to suffer from the aftermath of their absence, such as the rising heat. When we harm the earth, she will warn us. And if we continue harming her, she will certainly harm us. It was the first time I got handmade paper for a painting competition. Unfamiliar with its texture, I worried it would take me the whole day to finish the painting. Unwillingly, I had to return my sheet, which got an A-Grade later. The sea could not remain calm, and neither could I, inside that seaside abode! Somehow, I made myself sleep to get over the dissatisfaction of the day that had just ended.

The next morning, while going to the restaurant, we met a fisherman with his bicycle and a woven bamboo basket. He was going to the seaside to catch mussels with his net. After our breakfast, he appeared again. This time, his basket was full of mussels, which the people of Kannur used to call '*kallummakkaya*'.

We extended our stay in Kannur for two more days. In the evenings, we would go to the ice cream parlour by the beach, a little away from the Guest House. Lots of people would have taken over the beach by then: singles, couples, and families. Most would stay near the parlour. Some would sit on or walk among the rock formations scattered along the shore, savouring ice creams and gazing upon the sea, counting its infinite waves. The eccentric, adventure-loving few would brave the sea to climb the two massive, upright rocks that stood side-by-side in the water. In fact, the presence of people added to the beauty of the scenic setting. The Arabian Sea was in the ultimate phase of preparation to receive the setting sun. Sitting on the shore, I threw yesterday's unwanted baggage into her vastness. The waves caught it and pulled them offshore, to the deep zones of the seabed. "Now I can stay calm!" my mind whispered in relief. The cool breeze that came ashore brought new hopes.

Visiting St. Angelo's Fort (or Kannur Fort) was a totally unplanned decision. Built by the Portuguese Viceroy, Francis de Almeida, in the 16th century, captured and rebuilt by the Dutch in the 17th, and seized by the British in the 18th century, this laterite fort occupies a central place in the history of Malabar. It was obvious from the words of the security personnel how respected and celebrated this fort and its associations were in their minds. Measures of oppression and suppression under the colonialists are clear from the facilities provided in the fort. Inmates were confined to dark, cramped cells with insufficient headroom forcing them to sit or stoop. Our forefathers' determination and endurance yielded the freedom we enjoy today. The perforations in the laterite walls still echo the might of the foreign boots and the resistance offered by the brave freedom fighters. The half-lit passages in the fort opened up into vast courtyards, overlooking the sea.

We sat beneath a banyan tree on the raised platform built around it. While sitting there, we chanced upon a father and his little daughter sitting next to us. He came for a conversation with us. He was a teacher based in Thiruvananthapuram, who had come there for his wife's interview at a school for a teaching post. When he came to know that I was appearing for the Board exam of the tenth standard that year, he asked me whether I had started the preparations. I replied, "Not yet." As a teacher, he found my answer surprising because it was high time for students to begin their serious and rigorous preparations. He gave me tips to prepare systematically and to plan for the exams strategically. For me, the conversation was an eye-opening event; a spark of enlightenment beneath the banyan tree.

And that is life sometimes. Whenever we deserve and are destined to get or find something, it will come to us through its own means, be it through chance meetings with people, places, objects, incidents, or countless other ways. The law of attraction always works! They may present themselves as trifles or significant moments; it is up to us to find out what clue they offer. How well and for what purpose we use the chances and opportunities given or available to us at the moment decides the trajectory and pace of our growth.

Leaving the father-daughter duo and the fort, we spent that afternoon at the Parassinikkadavu Muthappan Temple and the Parassinikkadavu Snake Park. Snakes in this park occupied scattered and spacious enclosures. One of them was a wide and shallow well housing numerous snakes, where trained personnel would brief the spectators about the various snakes kept in it. In the show, they would explain the characteristics of various snakes, myths related to them, remedial measures like first aid for snakebites, etc. That evening, we visited the Payyambalam beach, where many rebellious and revolutionary souls rest in peace.

I returned home, reflective and determined. The next two months, I studied in a much smarter way, setting a study schedule for each day. I used to finish my exam papers in one to one-and-a-half hours, and the invigilators would look at me in wonder as I sat relaxed for the time remaining. During one exam, an invigilator even asked me to check the question paper again to see if I had missed anything.

My perception of Kannur changed following that visit. So too is the colour I once associated with it. Prejudices always create false perceptions unless we make a sincere effort to acquaint ourselves with and understand the ground realities. Now, I have given Kannur the colour blue; the blueness of sky and sea, of calmness, confidence, depth, heaven, stability, stillness, truth, and vastness.

7 ONE AMONG THE SIXTY GIRLS

To accept change has always been a tough task for me. To change my school, where I had been studying for ten years, was even tougher. It was with immense pain that I was transplanted to my new school, Cotton Hill Government Girls' Higher Secondary School in Vazhuthacaud, in the city of Thiruvananthapuram.

Cotton Hill School was established in the 19th century by the then ruler of Travancore, Maharaja Uthram Tirunal, as a free school for girls, in the present-day Government Sanskrit College in the city. A century later, it was moved to its present campus at Vazhuthacaud. It is one of the largest girls' schools in Asia. Although the rich legacy of the school inspired me a lot, I had a spiritless attitude towards it for no apparent reason.

Half-heartedly, I went to the new school on its reopening day, accompanied by my mother. After the first assembly on the very first day, I was in a real hurry to return home with her. Every day at school seemed bleak, and I attended it without my usual enthusiasm and energy. Many a day I was absent too—not only from the attendance register, but also in spirit.

I missed walking to my previous school, just one and a half kilometres from home. Each day offered something special. My sister would buy me new varieties of sweets and chocolates.

During heavy rains, we had to walk along the middle of the road, as the pedestrian path and one half of the road would be flooded with water. Speeding vehicles used to splash muddy water, drenching students wearing white and navy blue uniforms. It made me extra cautious during the rain. What really scared me was the series of buses, one after another, carrying the scientists and employees of the Indian Space Research Organization (ISRO) in Valiamala, located outside the city limits. They would whoosh by while I shuttled between home and school. Even now, my mother warns me to avoid that road, either on foot or in vehicles at times that coincide with the ISRO bus schedule. Episodes of fun and fear were part and parcel of those trips. Yet, I loved every bit of it.

The hardest part of the transfer to the new school was the horrible commuter stress I experienced while travelling on public transport. By the time the State Transport buses reached my bus stop, they would not halt because of the non-availability of space inside. Sometimes, I would not enter them, even if they halted, as they used to be tightly packed with people. On weekdays, in the mornings and evenings, the buses would be filled with people who depended on the city for their studies or work: students, parents, domestic helpers, employees, etc. Getting a seat was a luxurious privilege then.

The ladies-only bus that used to conduct a daily round-trip on that route, during school time, was a real lifesaver. It was deployed to serve several institutions in Vazhuthacaud, such as the Government Women's College, Music College, Cotton Hill School, and other colleges and schools en route. As it was not differentiated from other buses plying on the route, it looked identical to them, the only difference being the destination sign. This, unfortunately, almost always resulted in several funny incidents. Sometimes, when men stepped onto the first rung of the footboard without realizing it was a ladies-only bus, the girls and ladies erupted in laughter. It was a daily struggle; if I ever missed that bus, I had to take two or three connecting buses to get to school.

The Higher Secondary Block in the new school was on one of the highest points in the school campus, and one of the farthest too. This made me walk along the sloping terrain and climb a lot of steps. A final flight of steps leading to the Plus Two block lands at an open-to-sky court, lined by trees and surrounded by low-rise buildings. The Teaching block, the Administrative and Amenities blocks, are seen around the court in an anti-clockwise direction. High School classes neighboured ours, to the right, connected through open-to-sky courts of varying sizes. My first-year classroom was in the far-right corner on the second floor of the three-storey building.

I was worn out negotiating the school's undulating terrain and climbing the many steps all the way to my classroom. My health and energy were drained by the commuter stress induced by the miserable journey to and from school: the daily walk from my home to the bus stop, the journey in the fully loaded ladies-only bus, the walk from Vazhuthacaud bus stop to school, and from there to my class, and following the same procedure in the reverse order in the evenings.

My classroom had sixty girls. The strength of the class, classmates, and the class teacher would remain the same for the entire two years in Plus Two. My previous school was co-educational and there were roughly forty-five students in each class. My new school looked homogenous and monotonous because of a total lack of diversity. I often felt suffocated because of the disproportionate size of the classroom relative to the number of students. Though the strength of the class seemed unmanageable, the class teacher monitored each one of the sixty girls.

I used to gaze at the forecourt from the passage in front of my class. It was dotted with a lot of gigantic trees and short shade-giving ones. They were a great relief to me from the otherwise dull feeling I was undergoing in the initial days. The two-hour break on Fridays was yet another. During break times, High School girls wearing white shirts and green skirts could be seen amidst groups of Higher Secondary girls clad in green and white churidars. Whenever I felt fed up with my immediate surroundings, some classmates and I would stroll through the High School and Primary sections. During brief breaks, we would go to the canteen to have tea and *samosa*s, or to the store to buy lollipops. I received pocket money for my daily commute and for small treats like these. In the previous school, I never had to carry more than five or ten rupees, as there was hardly any need for it. Looking back, I realize that, unlike my peers, I was not good at money management. I would now advise school-going students to begin financial planning from a very young age.

To inculcate the habit of banking in school-going students, representatives from the State Bank of Travancore (later merged with the State Bank of India) came to our school. They helped students who were willing to open a savings account with their bank. I, too, started my first savings account, to which my scholarship amount in subsequent years got credited.

As each day passed, I was getting more comfortable with school. I kept on exploring my own moments of happiness there, and the results were promising as well. Gradually, my preconceptions proved wrong, and I started liking the school and treated it as mine too. It felt like a much bigger canvas for me to handle at the beginning. However, eventually, I managed to paint the entire picture, from parts to whole. For I learnt a lot from the two years spent in the new school with fifty-nine other girls in my class. I began to appreciate the diversity in my class: in terms of the environments they came from, their character, their understanding of and approach to different matters, and even their innocent smiles. I even made friends from high school, besides those from other streams in Plus Two. The bonds of friendship were strengthening, and so was my bond with the school.

Once, when I was hurriedly ascending the steps from the ground floor to reach my class, someone called my name from the nearby classroom. I stopped, and she came running to me and asked if I could remember her. Knowing that I really could not, she introduced herself, and I was quite surprised to find that she was my classmate in Kindergarten. We had parted more than a decade ago, and she could still recognize me in spite of the long interval. I have always been the same—then, now, and in all likelihood, in the future—as I have never been one to embrace change easily. Some evenings, teachers would ask students to perform their talents in the classroom. The sweet voices and melodious songs of my classmates still linger in my ears. I do not know how many times one of my friends, Lekshmi, had patiently sung the same song for me, upon my humble request.

When in need, my friends stepped up as my guides and moral supporters. Our casual talks during breaks often evolved into serious discussions on topics like gender equality, inequality, the role and contribution of women in society and economy. This does not mean that we were developing a so-called 'feminist' attitude, being in a girls' school. Rather, it made us realize who we were, what our actual strengths were, where we stood, and how to progress in this world with courage and confidence. I discovered that each one of us maintained a unique identity and personality in the same green and white coloured uniform.

As a premier institution under the Government of Kerala, our school was often the first to pilot new government schemes. Wherever opportunities seemed open, our teachers would motivate us to take part in them. We were encouraged to raise our voices in media debates on social causes. Movies and documentaries of value and societal importance were screened to improve our thought processes and to have a clearer, wider vision of the society that we have been a part of.

As time went on, I found pleasure in the daily commuting and even made friends in the ladies-only bus. The morning prayers sung by the students at school were so soothing, and they really helped me settle down after my arduous journey. During the walk to the bus stop in the evenings, I chanced to meet some of my old friends who were studying in the nearby schools. I engaged myself in various activities happening within and around my school. Not only did I attend events in school like Fresher's Day, Farewell, *Onam* celebrations, and Arts Festivals, but I also actively took part in them. When Tagore Theatre in Vazhuthacaud hosted the renowned arts festival and cultural event named Soorya Festival, I went there after school to see the exhibition and live paintings by artists.

In the second year, things became smoother, unlike in the first. My classroom was on the ground floor, which considerably reduced the number of steps I would otherwise have climbed. This allowed me to save a great deal of my energy.

To improve my performance in Computer Science, I joined a tuition centre with a few friends. After school, we would walk to the tuition centre, which was just four hundred metres away. Sometimes we took shortcuts through paths seldom used by others. On our way, we would 'invade' the Eastern bakery and have snacks and drinks. I always had tea or juice, and a butter bun with vanilla or chocolate filling.

Whenever we were tired, we would rest at the family office of our friend, which was usually unoccupied and en route to our tuition centre. On one such day, my friends thought of playing a trick on me. They all hid behind the kitchen when I was using the washroom, and I came out only to find none around. I kept calling their names while searching for them everywhere.

Reaching the kitchen, I could see a few shadows in motion through the translucent window. I knew it was them pranking me, and I could not help but laugh. And there ended their hide-and-seek game. They all came inside, and we all laughed at the failed 'conspiracy'.

After the tuition, my father would come and pick me up. We were regular customers at a vegetable shop in Vazhuthacaud. There I found some new varieties of bananas, which my father had never cultivated or bought before. Some days we would walk till the next junction of Vellayambalam, or take an auto to reach there. In that journey lasting about one and a half kilometres, we used to discuss several things like the happenings at school, new ideas and current affairs. What I value the most among the many things that I have learnt from Cotton Hill School is the virtue of being open-minded, through several means like observation, understanding, discourse, and experience.

Even after completing my Plus Two, I made occasional visits to Cotton Hill School. One of the public exams that I attended had its venue at Cotton Hill, and I decided to see my classroom once again. After the exam, I headed to the Plus Two block. The steep paths had been regraded into gentle slopes and finished with new flooring. The bare forecourt of my classroom has also been covered with floor tiles.

I did my B. Arch internship for six months at an office in Vazhuthacaud, located half a kilometre away from my school. That time, I used to take an auto from Vellayambalam and get off at the Vazhuthacaud bus stop. I chose to walk the rest of the way to my office enjoying the sight of young children and fondly reminiscing about my schooldays. All the while I walked past my school, I longed to walk along that stretch, wearing my green and white uniform, enjoying butter-buns, and playing hide-and-seek with my 'girls'.

8 GERMANY, IN MY MIND

Once, I attended the painting competition conducted by Goethe-Zentrum, the German Language Centre, at the Jimmy George Indoor Stadium in Thiruvananthapuram. Everyone was really excited about the prize awaiting the winner- 'An all-paid trip to Germany for a month!' 'Albert Einstein...Beethoven...Michael Schumacher...technological developments...I painted my ideas on the topic given to us, 'Germany, in my mind'. As usual, I finished my painting very early and began looking at my friends' works, admiring them.

Once the judge made his decision, we were all asked to assemble at the court for the result declaration. Leaving the gallery, I took a spot in the outer circle of those already assembled. They announced the names of the winners in reverse order: "Second runner-up...first runner-up..." Finally, the most awaited moment came. I remained calm, as I was never worried about the results. "And the winner is Jessin Kabir...!" I could not believe my ears! The judge, parents, and my friends applauded and congratulated me. One parent called my father, who was in his office, and told him, "Your daughter is going to Germany soon". The details of the contest appeared in newspapers, with some titled: "Schoolgirl on her way to Germany" and "Flights of

Fancy".

The Goethe Zentrum in Germany sent me a letter detailing the information and instructions regarding my trip and stay in Düsseldorf. It is a city in western Germany, lying on the banks of the Rhine River. I started visualizing the place from those descriptions, and the most exciting part was that the stay was to be in a hostel located beside the Rhine River. I began dreaming about the trip and even wished I could bring my vacation forward.

Meanwhile, I read books, watched travel videos then available on CDs, and gathered information from people about Germany, its culture, and its populace. Düsseldorf is the capital city of North Rhine-Westphalia, a state in Germany. The Düssel is a right tributary of the Rhine River, and Düsseldorf means 'the village of Düssel'. The city has a rich history and stood as a witness to both World Wars. The deeds of past dictators cast a long shadow on the nation. Some travelogues that I had gone through to familiarize myself with the place were also interested in providing a narrative of those deeds and their associated locations. Such facts and thoughts about Germany always disturbed me. Still, despite all these odds, it was definitely a dream trip for me. For I was travelling abroad for the first time, and it was my maiden trip by air. I continued dreaming day and night.

During the vacation that year, after completing my Plus Two, I joined the German language course, offered at no cost to me, being the first prize winner. The class was an assorted mix of people with different roles and goals, including teachers, doctors, IT professionals, a pastor, and those wanting to join their spouses in Germany. It is always good to learn a new language that is totally alien to us. It offers proven benefits, such as improved memory and brain development, enhanced relationships with people, and a deeper understanding and appreciation of the cultural traditions and nuances. Learning the basics of the language, I passed the beginners' course, named A1, with the grade *Gut*, meaning Good.

Putting an end to my long wait of about six months, I set out for my dream trip on 5th July 2009 from the Bengaluru Airport with my fourteen teammates from Delhi, Bangalore, and Hyderabad, and our team leader from Hyderabad. The flight took hours and hours to reach the transfer station at Frankfurt, in central Germany. Frankfurt is one of the largest cities in Germany, second only to Berlin, the capital. It is the birthplace of Johann Wolfgang von Goethe, a German writer and polymath, born in the 18th century. From there, we took another flight to Düsseldorf. While on the flight, I saw some students from Yemen who had also come for the same event hosted in another location. The delay in collecting our luggage made us wait a while at Düsseldorf Airport.

The organizers came to welcome and receive us at the airport. I sat in the back seat and fastened my seatbelt for the half-hour car journey. It took us along the beautiful streets of Düsseldorf and crossed the Rhine on the cable-suspended bridge named Rheinkniebrücke to reach our destination, the Jugendherberge (meaning Youth Hostel). The hostel was a minimalist grey building with glazed windows set in white frames. The premises had a lot of plants and trees, some with conical shapes, and some with spread-out foliage. To my surprise, I saw a maple tree, which until then I had only seen in books and movies. I looked for the Rhine River, and there it was, flowing beyond a beautiful meadow, across the road. The overall setting was almost similar to what I had visualized from the descriptions provided in the letter.

Outside the hostel, I saw a group of students from Africa. Some of them were playing table tennis, and some were sitting on the park benches, talking to each other. They were very nice to us. I called up my father and shared the first impression of the place and people I had come across till then.

In no time, the volunteers took us to our rooms. Mine had two bunk beds, study tables and chairs, an attached bathroom, and a toilet. Being alone in that room, the double-decker bunk beds reminded me of the concentration camps of the mid-20th century. Suddenly, someone entered the room. She was my roommate, Jona, from Taiwan. We greeted each other, introduced ourselves, and talked for a while, sitting around one table. Her real name was Wei Ting Hung, though Jona was much easier for me to pronounce. In the evening, the third one joined us: Ruth Munoz Escoto, from Mexico.

By evening, almost every participant had reached the hostel. There were altogether seventy-four students from fourteen different countries taking part in the PASCH-kurs Düsseldorf 2009, as the event was officially called. After the introductory session, the organizers wished us *Gute Nacht*, meaning Good Night. I found their farewell puzzling because it was still broad daylight outside. I could hardly believe that it was night already. Anyway, I turned my watch to suit the time zone in Germany.

The next day, the first session was our interview. I was the only one among our team who got admitted to class A2, officially called the 'Klasse: Heinrich Heine 2'. Christian Johann Heinrich Heine was the name of a 19th century German poet. Having shared a school bench with four or five others in the past, I had always longed for a seat of my own, like the one I had in kindergarten. Upon entering our respective classrooms the following morning, I was so happy to see the arrangement of my class; a flexible one with individual seats for each. Ms Grit Bertram was our teacher. Rather than encouraging English, she always replied pleasantly in German, which is a great way to learn a new language. In my class of sixteen including Ruth and me, there were students from Scotland, Egypt, Taiwan, and Uzbekistan. My other roommate, Jona, was in a higher grade.

Everyone there called me 'Yessin', since the German 'J' is pronounced like the English 'Y'. Likewise, 'Jona' was called 'Yona'.

We had a break in the forenoon itself. After having refreshments like fruits, snacks, and drinks, and talking to those from other classes, both happening in the common area, we would return to our respective classes. The three-and-a-half hour class was held only until noon. After that we had other activities conducted by the organizers, including painting, swimming, cycling, music, dance, movie screening, and hands-on workshops for crafts like face masks, ornaments, etc. It was during break times and these activities, that I met another set of friends; Amira, Shaimaa, Marina and Nada from Egypt, Best, Bee and Miew from Thailand (they went by short names, as their actual names are a bit difficult for others to use), Stephanie and Susana from Taiwan, Ivan and Pablo from Mexico, Aynur and Iroda from Uzbekistan, and many more. Through them, I was getting to know about their homelands too. In one of the painting workshops, Sarah, from Rwanda, Africa, became my art model. She really liked the portrait that I had sketched, and we became good friends.

On all Saturdays and on weekday afternoons, we visited nearby and far-off places with our programme volunteers. As we walked together, they would share experiences of their homeland. It was mandatory for male citizens to serve their nation by joining the military service whenever called for, and it became voluntary in 2011. Germans do value time, and they are very punctual. Once, when I was late by two minutes for the 9 o'clock class, the volunteers came in search of me and rushed me to the class.

There was an uninvited volunteer too, in all our visits: the rain in various forms, ranging from drizzle to downpours. Together, we explored nearly every part of Düsseldorf. The

Rheinkniebrücke and the Rheinturm are the two major architectural landmarks that stand out in the cityscape.

The Rheinkniebrücke (meaning Rhine Knee Bridge) is a cable-stayed bridge that connects us across the Rhine River to other parts of Düsseldorf, including the Altstadt, the Rheinturm, and beyond. It sits at a bend in the meandering Rhine—a curve that resembles a knee. The bridge accommodates six lanes for vehicles, with a combined cycle and footpath on either side.

The Rheinturm (the Rhine Tower) is a 240.5 metre high telecommunications tower located to the east of the Rhine River. It is the tallest building in the city of Düsseldorf, which has eventually contributed to the city's identity. It has a revolving restaurant and an observation deck on top of its shaft. Climbing atop the tower in the lift, I became speechless, for such was the view of the city from there. I got a bird's-eye view of the Rhine, the ships sailing through the river and those anchored at the docks, the Rheinkniebrücke, the green patches that adorn the city, the buildings around, the people and vehicles that were always in motion, and the rain-bearing clouds that were suspended from the sky. People could walk around an entire floor in the tower and enjoy the city's views through the slanting glass panes. My teammates from India urged me to join them in leaning back against the glass panes, saying, "Come on Jessin! You are the only person from Kerala! Give it a try at least." I humbly declined their offer. The glass might be toughened and has likely undergone safety testing before being installed there. Yet my mind was not tough enough to go for a crazy adventure that might cost my life.

The visit to the WDR studio, located near the Rheinturm, provided an overview of the history of radio broadcasting in Germany.

The walk along the streets of the Altstadt (meaning Old Town of Düsseldorf), in the drizzle, was an interesting one. I loved walking along the streets there, taking in the architecture, the people and their activities, and the shade under the trees and canopies of buildings. I particularly enjoyed the roses and other beautiful flowers in the landscaped areas, the street infrastructure, and the cleanliness of even the busiest streets. The positive environment offered by a state to its people pays off when they become responsible citizens, and they, in turn, enhance that environment for future generations, creating a virtuous cycle. I walked past many schools, libraries, art galleries and memorials. I took all these as inputs for my undergraduate programme in architecture, which was yet to begin in a month.

The Kunstmuseum (meaning art museum), located across the Rhine River, was an underground art museum. We spent much of our time viewing the works of artists and creating our own paintings.

The visit to Schloss Burg in Solingen (the 'City of Blades'), about twenty-five kilometres east of Düsseldorf, took an entire day. It is a castle originally built in the 12th century. There, I saw the military power and the centuries-old arms and armor of the Western world. The harshness of the Medieval era is evident in the fortified stone walls, the suits of armor worn by knights, the weapons used by the army, and the escape mechanisms installed in the castle. The castle, as it stands today, was conserved years after it had fallen into ruins.

The Xanten Archaeological Park, located about sixty-four kilometres north of Düsseldorf, was built on the site of the centuries-old Roman settlement in Germany. It is the largest open-air archaeological museum in the country. It showcases Roman cultural heritage, including an amphitheatre and a temple. The structures were reconstructed to show how the city might have been around two millennia ago. The apple trees that lined the park looked prettier in the evening drizzle.

The excursion to the Warner Brothers Movie Park was

another amazing experience. At the Film Museum, volunteers demonstrated various techniques and theories adopted in filmmaking, including flipbooks and the persistence of vision theory. They even made an instant film named 'Voyagers to Mars', with actors chosen from amongst us. In the amusement park there, I saw the group from Yemen, whom I had met on the flight from Frankfurt to Düsseldorf.

In the Aquazoo Löbbecke Museum in Düsseldorf, while I was looking at an aquatic species, my eyes chanced on a lady who had been gazing at me for a considerable time. On account of her appearance, she strongly resembled people from Kerala. Even so, people from other countries do sometimes look like us, say, for example, those from Sri Lanka. Hence, I tried to ignore her looks and move on. In another exhibition space, I noticed she was still following me with her eyes. Suddenly, she said something randomly. I wondered if she shared my curiosity regarding my place of origin. To get off her radar, I broke the ice by replying to her in Malayalam, "Entho?" meaning 'Yes'. Excitedly, she replied, "I knew you were a *Malayali* (Keralite)!" Having been relieved of the awkward situation, we smiled at each other and introduced ourselves. She asked me if I liked the food provided at the youth hostel. I told her that I had been eating only light food and fruits. Then she made an instant offer to me, "Shall I cook rice for you and bring it to your place?" I thanked her for being so generous, but humbly turned it down, as we had to follow the rules of the camp, and also I did not want to bother her.

While travelling around, I realized the advantage of having learnt German. We were always instructed to move in groups and to carry maps whenever we stepped out of the hostel. And my teacher had already taught us the essential words and phrases for navigation. One day, I went out with some friends. Due to some emergency, I had to return to the hostel alone. I sought help from passersby by pointing to my destination on the map, allowing me to find my way back. They were all surprised to hear me speak German so fluently and were amazed that I had picked it up in just two months.

Reaching the metro station, I asked a gentleman where I could collect the tickets from. He took me upstairs and helped me get my tickets from the vending machine. When the train came, both of us rushed down and entered it. He asked about my reasons for visiting Germany and was pleased to hear my story. I thanked him for his help; he just smiled. When the train was about to reach another station, he said, "That is where you have to get down. Walk straight ahead, and then take a right turn to reach your hostel". I thanked him again with a smile, wished him a happy journey ahead, and got off the train. Following his words, I walked straight, took a turn in the street, and saw the board 'Jugendherberge'. I could not control my happiness. Singing songs and dancing lightly along the street, I headed towards my hostel. I thanked God for keeping track of me and sending me the right people to show me the right path in tough times.

As the youth hostel was open to the public, many depended on it for food, accommodation, and entertainment. Sometimes, families would gather on the premises to hold a get-together. Couples, irrespective of their age and health, would sing and dance together. They illustrated how beautifully life can be celebrated.

Whenever I had free time, especially in the evenings and on Sundays, I would go down to the Rhine. A road ran along the east side of the Youth Hostel, flanked by a thick green blanket of lawns and lush meadows bordering the river. I would sit on a park bench by the road, simply enjoying the beauty of the river and the city skyline, defined by the cables and towers of the Rheinkniebrücke, and the shaft and the decks of the Rheinturm, soaring in the sky. Adults of all ages would go for evening walks, with their cute puppies and giant dogs, on harnesses and leashes. Once, a jogger wearing headphones passed by and waved at me. Rabbits emerged in large numbers as evening fell. Whenever I tried to catch one, they would scurry away to hide in the nearby bushes. Lambs and flocks of sheep sometimes appeared on the meadows. White birds would fly from the riverbank towards the blue sky. After moments of stillness, the river's waters would be churned by speeding boats and giant ships that sailed through it. The Rhine, truly, was a visual treat!

For the 'International Abend' (meaning International Evening), we staged the cultural programmes unique to each country. It was an evening where course participants would celebrate and honour their homelands. The team from India made a brief presentation on the diversity of Indian culture. Later, I recited a poem in Malayalam (my mother tongue) written by Changampuzha Krishna Pillai, a 20th century poet from Kerala. I learnt the poem by overhearing my sister's teacher reciting it in class.

The three-week course of A2 ended with an exam, and I passed with flying colours, bagging the grade *Sehr Gut* (meaning Very Good). On the last day, we had a grand farewell party and a feast as part of the certificate distribution for the various levels of the German language course. Prior to everyone's departure, there was a fireworks session as well. As we had to leave early for the airport, I packed my luggage and got dressed in advance. Everyone was enjoying the fireworks outside, and I thought of lying down on my bed for a while. Unfortunately, I fell fast asleep. After a while, I sensed someone touching me gently, and instantly I opened my eyes. That was Lucie, a volunteer at the camp. Realizing I had woken up abruptly, she held my hands and whispered, "Wake up, it's time for you to depart."

9 THE OASIS IN JAISALMER

Preconceptions and prejudices are inherent to human nature. I too had and still have many biases of different sorts, and one of them was regarding hot deserts and the life over there. Besides having a hot and arid climate, I thought desert life was scary and exhausting. Such were the visualizations I had captured from books and movies, most of which portrayed and highlighted the dilemmas and tragedies occurring in the sand, burning under the scorching sun. Thankfully, there were some promising visuals too: the green patch of oasis in a dreary desert that shades and shelters many beings; the camels that 'ship' people and their goods across the shifting sandy dunes; and cactus plants that adapt to the harsh climate via their leaves, stems, and roots. Yes, deserts teach us a great lesson—the lesson of perseverance and endurance.

I wished to be in a hot desert, at least for a short while, watching the sand dunes and the occasional winds that streamline them, the voyage of the caravans of people with their camels and goods, the innocent smiles on the veiled faces of ladies, wearing large white bangles, who cover long distances with pots of water stacked on their heads, and so on.

The Thar Desert, also called the Great Indian Desert, is the hottest desert in India (Ladakh being the coldest). A major part of it lies in the Indian state of Rajasthan. My wish to visit a hot desert was fulfilled with the All India Tour in 2013, as part of my undergraduate studies. Unanimously, we planned to tour the northern and western parts of India. And Rajasthan got a prime place in the itinerary, with visits scheduled to Jaisalmer and Jodhpur. Two days were set aside to explore Jaisalmer, located entirely in the desert.

We travelled on a bus from Ahmedabad in Gujarat to Jaisalmer in Rajasthan. The overnight journey on the upper deck of the bus's sleeper coach made me feel as if I were floating on water. The next day, early in the morning, we reached Jaisalmer. Though not fully awake, I could see everyone slowly alighting the bus. I moved the curtains aside and looked out of the window. A nearly leafless tree; cattle loitering about, some resting on ground covered in cow dung; old men, wearing long white shirts with coats, dhotis and headgears, sitting in circles and in series, shoulder to shoulder, some supported by long wooden sticks; buildings in yellow sandstone; a setting I had till then seen only in paintings and movies portraying village life of Rajasthan. That was an impressive scene to start my day in Jaisalmer, 'the Golden City' in the heart of the Thar Desert. I stepped off the bus into overwhelming hues of yellow, with shades ranging from the bright lemon of sunrays to the warm ochre of sandstone.

We checked into the hotel and unloaded our luggage. The rooms were arranged on both sides of a narrow corridor lit by a skylight in the roof. As I approached my room, I spotted a blue patch in the distance. It was an open-to-sky swimming pool. I entered my room, which had already become an oven. Bathing was of no use in the sauna-like bathroom. After a very spicy breakfast at the hotel, we set out for the first port of call, the living Golden Fort. It was within walking distance of our hotel.

As we walked along the sloping royal road to the fort gate,

shopkeepers invited us towards their shops, located beside the road. Embroidered cloth bags, beautifully printed kurtas and skirts, and other colourful handicrafts that are native to Rajasthan caught my eye, as I had mostly been seeing hues of yellow since the dawn of that day. I did not stop by the shops, as I could not wait to see the fort that adorned the hilltop.

Jaisalmer translates to 'the fort of Jaisal'. Jaisal Singh was the ruler who, in the 12th century, built this fort and founded the new capital for his state, both named Jaisalmer. This is a hill fort in desert terrain, occupying the summit of Trikuta Hill, and defended naturally by the desert landscape that surrounds it. It is built of yellow sandstone, which is an abundant local resource in Jaisalmer. Considering all these, the Jaisalmer Fort is also called Trikutgarh, Swarn Durg, Sonar Quila, or the Golden Fort. It is one among the six forts in Rajasthan inscribed as a UNESCO World Heritage Site in 2013, under the name 'The Hill Forts of Rajasthan'.

The architecture of the fort trumpets the power and glory of the erstwhile Rajput princely state of Jaisalmer. Its thick walls, strengthened by bastions on which were kept the cannons, the battlements (parapets with regularly spaced squared openings), merlons (*kanguras*), balconies (*jharokas*), among others, show the defensive measures adopted for fort-building during the medieval period. The Rajput style of architecture drew inspiration from antecedents and neighbours (Sultanate and Mughal), and influenced later regional styles of architecture, such as Maratha. Besides the royal palace called Raj Mahal, the fort encloses Jain temples, urban centres, havelis of wealthy merchants, and residences of common people.

The architecture of the fort and its component buildings exemplifies how built structures can adapt to an arid climate by integrating vernacular architecture and traditional knowledge systems. Jaisalmer is located entirely in the desert, where the sun is relentless and water is scarce. The design of buildings and open spaces, thus, had to ensure user comfort by screening the sun to the greatest extent possible. Small openings, perforated screens like *jali*s, courtyards, buildings in close proximity, open spaces, and streets shaded by nearby buildings were some measures adopted to deal with the blazing heat. A guide explained the methods of water management in practice several centuries ago. Efficient use of water was a necessity, and people took great care not to waste even a single drop of it.

After seeing the Raj Mahal, we continued walking within the fort. As time went on, the number of visitors to the fort kept increasing. We passed through a chowk that was occupied by singers, vendors, visitors, cattle, cars and a big banyan tree. Tempted by the colourful braided turbans on display, I bought one and put it on. We walked further along the streets, seeing the marvels finely crafted in yellow sandstone: the Jain temples, havelis, and houses.

It is a living fort, as it accommodates the descendants of families that have been living inside it for several centuries. The living urban settlement and the Jain temples that the fort encloses make it a unique example of a secular (urban) and sacred fort. When the fort could no longer house the growing population, the spillover of the excess ones resulted in the settlement outside the fortification, which later rose as a town at the base of the Trikuta hill. UNESCO notes that certain types of urban development in the surrounding town could pose a threat to the wider setting and the views to and from the fort. It was also found that the fort has development pressures, as encroachments and enlargements, and the hill has been under the threat of water seepage because of infrastructural incapacity.

By then, the midday sun had exhausted us all, signalling a need for food. Even though a bit late for lunch, we could find a nice rooftop restaurant. A single staff member was responsible for taking orders, serving food, and entertaining guests. That multitasking man gave the kitchen staff, instructions for the food we ordered. Since they served only freshly cooked food, we waited more than half an hour for it to reach our table. While we waited, he entertained us with tales of the beauty and valour of the royals of Raj Mahal. He told us that their 'Raja' (the incumbent Rajput ruler in the palace) was the most handsome person he had ever seen. After lunch, we took a rickshaw to see the Raja at his Mandir Palace, which they had converted into a heritage hotel. Unfortunately, he was away on a foreign tour. From there, in another rickshaw, we moved to the third destination of the first day, Gadisar Lake.

The Gadisar Lake is an artificial rainwater lake excavated in the 12th century. It was rebuilt in the 14th century by Gadsi Singh, after whom it has been named. It had been the sole water source of the city for many years until other sources were developed. There were ghats, temples and pavilions (*chhatris*) around it.

It seemed the evenings in Jaisalmer were also unbearably hot. Dehydrated as well as drained of energy and enthusiasm, we bought and emptied bottles of water one after the other. As we were approaching the lake, my apprehensions gradually evaporated. I sat beneath a tree by the lake, facing it. The water was still, reflecting whatever stood within and around it. A breeze passed by, gently touching the lake, making ripples and waves in its waters. Far away, the sun was setting in the hillocks on the plains; the yellow shades gradually turned into shades of red and blue. The weather was getting milder with a drop in temperature. The ghats became deserted, and we returned to the hotel.

When the whole of Jaisalmer fell asleep, the entire class walked along its veins towards Gadisar Lake, which was about a mile away from the fort. We sat down at the ghats and in the chhatris. The water was stagnant, reflecting the moon and millions of stars in the dark blue sky.

The next forenoon was spent visiting various havelis—the residences of the nobility and rich merchants—including the Moti Mahal (Salam Singh ki Haveli) and the Patwa Haveli. They showcase wall paintings, intricate and unique stone lattice work (*jali*), priceless artefacts, and the interplay of light and darkness through the well-lit and ill-lit spaces. The fluttering and chirps of bats and pigeons inside created a sense that these were 'living havelis'. Walking up to the terrace of one haveli, I looked through a frame in the perforated parapet. The fort crowned the slopes of Trikuta Hill, with the town spreading downhill, resembling an anthill. The built heritage of the town, crafted in yellow sandstone, seemed to merge together, apparently making it difficult to distinguish and discern where one structure ended and another began.

While wandering the narrow, winding streets, residents sitting on their doorsteps would invite us for a cup of tea with a sincere smile. The way-side vendors and souvenir shop owners eagerly vied for our attention. Sometimes the wandering cattle would scare us at the turns in the streets. The shade and seating provided by the buildings lining the streets offered us relief in the desert city. Conserving the fort and its environs would have been a daunting task had it not been for the residents who took pride and ownership in their heritage.

Tourism has become a major economic mainstay for the people and the place, both of which traditionally thrived on a caravan-led economy which depended on the land routes through the desert. Jaisalmer has been through droughts, famines, and other economic hardships throughout its history. In spite of all that, it thrived, with the sheer determination of the people who refused to succumb to difficulties that arose time after time. The beauty that Jaisalmer offers to the spectators is born from the willpower of those who chose to survive.

After lunch, our bus took us outside the fortified town to a stretch of barren land for the desert safari. I saw camels, their cameleers and guides in large numbers. As soon as I got off the bus, one cameleer grabbed my hand and tried to pull me. I shouted at him to get his hand off me. I was shocked to find how they were soliciting clients! After the initial commotion for a few minutes, the spot and the scene settled down. Two people had to ride on each camel. For our safety and to balance the load on the poor camels, we paired up a light person with a relatively heavier one. Once everyone had achieved equilibrium, the camels began to move.

On our way, one of my friends, mounted on a camel and riding alongside me, joked that the guides might take us to Pakistan. Though a joke, I could not dismiss it entirely, as about fifteen percent of the Thar extends into the territory of Pakistan, separated by the Radcliffe Line. I looked at our guide, who seemed to be a rough person. I grew apprehensive and stayed alert, ensuring that my friends were riding on the camels either ahead of or behind mine.

A wind blew, laden with sand and heat, and I closed my eyes to let it gently pass through. It embraced me by dropping sand all over my body. I knew it was a welcome gesture from the Great Indian Thar Desert!

Like the illusion created by the yellow sandstone, back in the city, the yellow sand, the camels, all seemed to merge with each other, the only difference being the colours that clothed people, and the blue sky. The skyline of the city was static, with sharp angular edges and bold lines that were either straight or curved. Whereas the skyline in the desert featured free-flowing lines. Its shape and location changed constantly, depending on the direction and intensity of the wind.

The slow-footed camels, which were moving together in groups, gradually followed a line of path, leaving deep impressions of their footprints behind. Their humps moved up and down as the passengers swayed and toed and froed in slow motion, their rhythm perfectly matching that of the camels. The four-legged camels, the two-legged cameleers, and the people cruising on the camels cast their shadows on the sand, like the characters and properties shown in a shadow theatre. I got the impression that I was moving with a desert caravan.

Reaching the end of the trail, everyone assembled at a common place. The camels sat on the sand, and travellers dismounted from them. If anyone wished to go for a race and was ready to pay the cameleers an extra amount of money, the same camels would be readied. I thought of going for a race on my camel. Unfortunately, that naughty and disobedient being was lurching upward instead of trotting calmly. When the cameleer-boy started beating it, I told him not to and to drop me right away. I guess the arid climate and the interaction with other cameleers and such mischievous camels might have made him aggressive at this very young age. To let him calm the animal, I walked back to the end of the trail.

A lot of activities were going on there that evening. Some men, in their traditional dresses, were singing and playing instruments, and little girls were dancing to the beats of that music. The musicians kept on singing folk songs, which sounded like a lullaby for the setting sun. I have seen the Sun 'setting in the seawater'. This was the first time I was seeing it 'setting in the desert sand'. The heat in the desert was slowly subsiding. As the caravan departed, the desert was deserted again. Post the desert safari, we left for our desert camp.

In our camp, women dressed as dancers welcomed us. Upon reaching the open court, we encircled the performers, who entertained us with songs and dances. The entire night was steeped in their performance. After having dinner, I went to our hutment, built to resemble a traditional hut. The unit where I stayed had a bedroom and an attached bathroom. As I did not want to sleep that night, I went out to sit by the campfire; all of us sang our favourite songs together. After sometime I left the campfire for a stroll.

In the hours that followed, until dawn, I walked along the boundary of our camp, looking up and down, and far beyond. The yellow sand felt cool, as did I. My thirst for water disappeared, and I felt lighter. The moon and innumerable glittering stars adorned the dark blue sky. I could feel the existence of all three forms of matter at once: solid sand beneath, liquid me in between, and gaseous sky above. My mind whispered, "You have found the oasis! Let's stay here forever."

10 THE SCHOOL OF MY LIFE

Dreams once seeded, yet long-forgotten, can come true, accidentally as well. The wish I had made at the National Bal Bhavan (NBB) had been searching for me for six long years. Somewhere in my Bachelor of Architecture journey, I considered pursuing a Master's in Architectural Conservation, rather than practicing immediately after completing my degree. After engaging in discussions with my professors and experts in the field, I sent my application to the School of Planning and Architecture (SPA), New Delhi. I worked day and night to prepare my portfolio and was confident I would be accepted after the interview. My intuition proved right, and I secured my admission to the SPA.

Knowing this, people who loved me were quite happy to see me studying there. They were equally anxious about how secure I would be in that capital city, especially after the 'Nirbhaya' case. Unlawful activities and deeds of a few can blight a city's image by assigning wrong notions to them. "But it's Delhi, which gave me a title and an identity! I'll be safe there. I must go!" I convinced myself with this assertion, and with courage and confidence, packed my bag and started my journey to Delhi in July 2014. My parents joined me on that trip.

My seven-month-old nephew came to the railway station with his parents to see us off. He was all happy and giggling and was trying to say something. We knew he wanted to come with us. The train left the station, and we waved at them. There were tears in everyone's eyes, except in the eyes of that innocent kid, which sparkled with joy. I have been to several places since a young age and have stayed away from home for several days and weeks. Still, this trip seemed different, and I could sense that, as everyone did. This time, I had to stay away; not for some days or weeks, but for months totaling two years. I realized I was going far away from my home, in space and time; the homesickness in me was awakened. My friend, Dr Niyati, told me she used to get nostalgic while journeying back to Delhi by train through the extensive paddy fields in Palakkad. It was a feeling every traveller might have while leaving their home behind. Seeing the paddy fields in Palakkad, I was reminded of her words.

It took just two nights and two days to reach Delhi. The weather was pleasant, as the summer had drawn to a close. The first two days were consumed by the admission procedures, orientation sessions, fee payments, procedures to avail the hostel room and mess coupons, and miscellaneous other things. I met my classmates and roommates, Ruchita and Sneha, who had already settled into college life. Both of them were from Maharashtra, one from Pune and the other from Thane.

The girls' hostel is within the college campus itself, and it was hardly five metres away from the academic block. Boys stayed at SPA's residential campus hostel in Maharani Bagh, known as MB, about 10 kilometres away. To get into the hostel, one had to rank in the top three academically. The initial admission was also based on academic merit and an interview.

I took a quick look inside the hostel. The three-storey building was planned around a central courtyard, with rooms arranged around it. Every room opened onto a passage or a corridor. Two such passages on opposite sides faced the courtyard, while two others did not. Of the remaining two passages, one overlooked a gym and play court, and another was a corridor with rooms on one side and a perforated brick wall on the other, because of its nearness to the academic block. My room was along the passage that fronted the courtyard. Its balcony looked out onto the forecourt of the college. I checked my room and made a list of essentials I would need to make the space comfortable. To buy essentials from that checklist, I went with my parents to the nearby market called Laxmi Nagar. The next day, I had to join my classes, and my parents had to leave for Kerala.

That day, being my first day, they came to college with me and waited until I had finished my breakfast. It was almost time to reach my class, which would commence at 9 AM. We exchanged hugs and kisses, and with a heavy heart, they left me, and I broke into tears. I stood still as tears rolled down my cheeks. My friends immediately took me to class. I accepted the fact that from then on, I was on my own and had to manage everything myself.

The classes went fine, and that afternoon, in our studio, we formed different groups to study different areas of Delhi. I, along with my two roommates, formed the group that was to study the Qutb Complex and Mehrauli in South Delhi. That same afternoon, we set out from the college and walked to Pragati Maidan, and took the metro to Mehrauli. The ITO metro station, around 300 metres away from our college, popped up only in our second year. From Mehrauli, we took an auto to the Qutb Complex. I asked the auto-driver to go slowly as he was driving rashly. With one leg crossed over the other, he was looking here and there, but certainly not at the road. Seeing me grow frustrated by his reckless driving, Ruchita and Sneha could not stop laughing. Somehow, we reached our destination safely! This was the second time I had seen the Qutb Complex. The first was when I had come for the interview a few months back. The Qutb complex comprises the Qutb Minar, the Quwatul Islam Mosque, Alai Darwaza, Iltutmish's Tomb, Alai Minar and much more. We did a quick reconnaissance survey of the Qutb Complex and left for other areas of Mehrauli in the evening.

On the way, both of them were excited to find a lady selling street food in front of Jahaz Mahal. To them, the fried *pakoda*s, *golgappa*s, and lime that they had from there were absolutely mouthwatering. I refused their offer to have any, as I was extremely worried about my health vis-à-vis street food. I kept checking my watch and was getting anxious as I was supposed to get back to the hostel by 6 PM because of the 'curfew' imposed by my parents. However, we could reach the hostel only at around 8 PM.

That night, I took my clothes and buckets to the washroom to wash. A friend of mine taught me how and when to use detergent and soap. I bent down to wash and realized how painful it was to wash clothes manually. I wept, but blamed none, as studying there was my choice. After all, one has to do their chores oneself.

The second day, at the mess hall, I sat in front of my breakfast: three slices of brown bread, two scoops of butter, half a teaspoonful of jam just to give it a cherry red colour, a bowl of milk with cornflakes, and a cup of tea. As I gazed at it for a while, tears fell from my eyes. At home, my mother would chase me to feed me breakfast. At the mess, nobody was there to insist or urge us to either have or finish our food. For the two years spent in Delhi, I strictly stuck to this breakfast diet, nothing more and nothing less. The only exception was when a dessert like *kheer* (rice pudding) replaced cornflakes or when the entire menu was replaced by *puri* and its 'associates', which had happened only in the rarest of cases. Following a diet certainly helped me sustain myself until I returned home.

The timing of the lunch was a bit disappointing, as the mess would open only at 1 PM, which I was unaccustomed to until then. I was used to having lunch at exactly 12 noon—a schedule established by my previous institution. To fit the new institution's schedule, I had to reset my biological clock. Some Saturdays, randomly, we could have *masala-dosa* for lunch. The mess would be exceptionally crowded on those days. Besides all these, the mess remained closed for dinner every Saturday. Either we had to dine out or place an order for doorstep delivery. Some invested their time to prepare food, which they lovingly shared with others as well.

On their return trips from Kerala, after vacations or personal leave, my friends would bring meals wrapped in plantain leaves and other special recipes prepared at their homes. Whenever I felt sick of the mess's food, the Kerala House canteen and my local guardian's home came to my rescue. Upon arriving home for my first holidays, I strictly removed certain foods from my diet: bread, *puri*, potato, *dal*, and green peas.

The other canteen near our hostel and mess served light refreshments. It was closed on weekends, making Saturday evenings even more difficult. A small store run by an old man and his son, near the In-gate of the campus, sold machine-tea, snacks, and packaged foods. Another shop named Safal, located outside the rear gate, sold fruits and dairy products. Both establishments were lifesavers, especially during exams and holidays. It was only in our second year that a small coffee shop opened on campus, right in front of our hostel.

The proximity of the hostel to the academic block was advantageous in the sense that it offered extra time to devote to the needs of the hour, either to rest or to work. Savings in time were indeed a solace to me. Having travelled ninety minutes each way daily during my higher secondary and undergraduate studies, I am well aware of how terrible commuter stress can be. For me, another advantage of staying in a hostel was that the senior students and other expert and smart friends were handy whenever I was in trouble or had a serious problem or query to be solved instantly. These interactions included solving software doubts, using new data analysis tools, navigating city services, and finding essential shops. In every case, I received sound advice and valuable guidance on matters both large and small. Furthermore, I simply liked spending time with them.

Certain matters remained unresolved, requiring my attention and immediate resolution. In the initial days at college, I could not concentrate on personal or professional matters. Studies, duties, everyday tasks, and chores—everything seemed tedious, repetitive, and even uninteresting. In addition, I found myself slower than my peers at almost all activities. I began finding reasons for this, ranging from my priorities to my steadfast habit of choosing the 'hard path' over working smart. Eventually, I realized that comparing myself with others was futile, serving only to drain my time and energy. Thereafter, I decided to give myself time to find a genuine, doable solution. That was when I started observing the individuals around me.

Slowly, I realized that proper management of things and multi-tasking, and above all, remaining cool is the success mantra to get through. To put these into practice, one has to know who one is, one's own strengths and weaknesses, and what one can and cannot do. Fortunately, I realized I had been living in a self-scripted comfort zone. I had been unnecessarily confining and controlling myself, which had long hindered my growth. Once I started listening to and following what my mind had to say, things became easier and more manageable. Slowly, everything fell into place at the hostel, in my class, and in my whole life. I noticed I was starting to enjoy whatever I was doing, be it having breakfast, washing clothes, or studying.

There was an informal group of students from SPA Delhi from Kerala, named 'SPAdikam'. The first meeting of

'SPAdikam' was held in the garden inside Feroz Shah Kotla. On that wintry November night nine years ago, I was unaware of the historical significance of the place where I had landed. Both the National Bal Bhavan (NBB) and the SPA Delhi are at a walkable distance from the remnants of what was the historic fortified city of Firozabad. The city was built by Feroz Shah Tughlaq, the medieval ruler who ruled over the Sultanate of Delhi in the 14th century. Feroz Shah Kotla was the fortress built by him for his city, which encloses an Asokan Pillar, a Jami Masjid, and a *Baoli* (well). Thus, the name 'Kotla Road' for the road that abuts the NBB.

Within a few weeks, senior students invited the new joiners in the respective departments to attend the Fresher's Day functions, held in a mini hall at the MB hostel. From the firsthand accounts of our hostel mates who already had their functions, and from my personal experience, I came to know that those were the opportunities for the senior students and the newcomers to get to know each other, their backgrounds and talents, though briefly. They differed from the disturbing episodes of ragging that, unfortunately, continue to happen in some institutions despite being banned by law. Such practices violate all ethics, humanity, and most of all, common sense. The 'curfew' was broken again on our Fresher's Day. Since the function started late, we returned to our hostel late at night, but in groups. Delhi, or any other place, is safe as long as we remain alert and travel in groups of known people, and get a thorough understanding of the area we are travelling through.

The academic calendar of SPA used to be published well in advance. It gave a clear picture of holidays, exam dates, and above all, the winter and summer vacations, both of which had a longer duration between semesters. The college strictly followed it, no matter what happened. I was impatiently waiting to go home on the first set of holidays. And within three months of joining the first semester, *Pooja* holidays arrived, and I caught my flight home. I reached home with a handful of wishes, which were to be fulfilled before going back to Delhi, and a headful of work, which was to be accomplished within a month after the holidays.

But the very first task, upon reaching home, was predetermined, which was to see my little nephew. I found happiness in tracking his developments, even from a far-off place. His first birthday was just a month away, and I knew it would be celebrated in my absence. Once, while I was watching devotees singing *bhajan*s (hymns) at the ISKCON temple, Sneha came running towards me, as if she had made a discovery! She asked me to go with her quickly, and I was wondering why she was so excited. She grabbed my hand and took me to a stall selling souvenirs and curios. Pointing to a kurta and pyjama, she said, "Hey, buy this, this will be perfect for your nephew". Packing it with other gifts I had in store for him, I posted it home to gift him on his first birthday. While cutting the cake, he wore the outfit that I had gifted him. Though I missed his second birthday too, I never forgot to send him gifts that were carefully curated and handcrafted by me.

During the rest of my vacation, I finished my academic tasks, even though there was still time left for their submission after the vacation. The hard worker in me thought of finishing those tasks peacefully at home, rather than rushing them amidst other things in Delhi. I used to count down the days until the return date. With a heavy heart, I took my flight back to Delhi. I always chose flights, as travelling by train would have consumed at least five full days for a round-trip. That would have shortened a vacation already loaded with academic work. Thus, flight journeys consumed a major part of my GATE scholarship.

The cool breeze that blew on some nights informed me of winter. But we were facing the 'heat' of the final jury of our studio project. The first semester exams started in December. At SPA, exams were never nightmares, having once even written three papers in three hours. We wrote the semester-end exams in extreme climates; the first and third semester exams during winters, wearing gloves; and the second and fourth semester exams during summers, wearing half or shorter sleeves. I loved the one in winter the most. The exam venue was on the nearby campus of SPA, which houses the undergraduate programme. It is located about 600 metres north of our college, on the way to Feroz Shah Kotla. On those winter mornings, I would walk along the tree-lined avenue, backpack on my shoulders and a book in my hand, humming winter songs, and dancing gently to their rhythm. I saw how winter manifested itself in its many forms, in Delhi.

Hostel life was the most exciting part of my SPA days. I had lived in two rooms in the hostel, one each year. Both of them had three beds, a built-in shelf, an almirah, a study table and a chair. My first room on the second floor had the added advantage of a balcony, long but narrow, overlooking the front yard of the college. From there, we could, to a small extent, track the activities on the campus, and also of the road in front of the college. The second room was on the third floor, to the rear of the hostel, which did not have a balcony. From here, we could only see our roommates and the ones passing along the corridor, and the happenings on the terrace on the same floor, and of the courtyard as seen from the passage in front of the room. I could see my second room from the stair landing of the academic block. Both rooms were small, yet we each had our own space; I had a bed, a shelf and a foldable table that could be placed on the bed, the rest being under collective ownership. In fact, everyone lived in their own little world happily, sharing and caring for others as well.

Whenever I felt bored or sad, I would go to my friends, talk to them for a while, or go for a walk within the campus and get refreshed. In the second semester, my classmate, Sudipta, was also there in the hostel. Whenever I visited her room, she would prepare instant tea for us. Sipping it, we would discuss the progress of our documentation of Madhi Masjid in Mehrauli. Her roommate, who closely watched our interactions, used to call me 'Boss'! The night before exams, she would teach me the concepts clearly and give me printouts of notes from her personal printer.

It was my classmate, Neelima, who introduced me to what was called 'Korean Drama'. The night she invited everyone to her room to celebrate her birthday, she really regretted having given me a series from her personal collection. For, while everyone else was in a celebratory mood, I was the only one sitting on her bed, watching the last episodes of that drama on my laptop, with tears in my eyes. From then on, I stopped watching anything that made me emotional. Someone once told me they never paid to watch movies that would make them sad.

Apart from humans, there were pigeons, cats, dogs, and squirrels too on our campus. I hardly found any crows there. At the most unexpected moments, a troop of monkeys, ranging from newborns to 'senior citizens', would barge into our hostel. They used to invade the common spaces, walk along the corridors and on the handrails of the stairs. Sometimes they would enter the rooms and inspect them casually, like a hostel warden, as if they were in charge then. Newborns would cling to their mother's body, while the latter kept moving around. The little ones would hang from the railings and play with the horizontal iron bars, like acrobats using a trapeze. Their surprise visits to our hostel shook up our routines completely. Their parades during the morning rush hour were particularly chaotic, when students were in a real hurry to get ready for classes. Some get stuck in the washroom, and some in their rooms. Girls would scream for help when the monkeys threw their fully dried clothes onto the wet and dusty sunshades and in the courtyard. I could not control myself from laughing, looking at a monkey playing with someone's white pants, which ultimately turned brown when dirtied. That was the naughtiest monkey I had ever seen.

I, too, had an encounter with a monkey outside my first room at the hostel. I was going to the washroom next door, and while opening my door, I chanced upon a monkey in the passage. It was feeding on a packet of leftover food on a table placed between my room and the washroom. To shoo it away, I waved my hands at it, which was more than enough to provoke that short-tempered being. Angrily, it screeched and jumped towards me. Had I not grabbed the lever of my room's door, I would have become a 'martyr' of deadly monkey attacks in the hostel.

Besides this, I had a terrible experience with a cat. One morning, a cat had trespassed into the same room. As instructed, it got out of the room obediently. After lunch, when I came back to my room, I saw the same cat peacefully resting on my bed. Seeing me glaring at it, the cat fled the room in no time. I started cleaning the area where it was sleeping, only to find that the mischievous cat had urinated there before fleeing. That night, I had to sleep on my bare cot because I had kept the mattress on the terrace for drying after many cycles of washing. After that incident, I never trifled with animals again.

From my first day of college, I saw two dogs named 'Shahrukh' and 'Laila' being cosseted and petted by the students of SPA. Rarely had I seen them entering the hostel. As the students played with these dogs, a little white puppy with a muddy body would eagerly peek through the bottom rail of the college gate, seeking attention. He would have been jealous of the way the other two were taken care of. Neelima was once delayed on a trip to Bhangarh in Rajasthan, well before sunrise, because he was playing with her and blocking her path. He did the same to me, too, when I was hurrying to the National

Archives. An auto-driver near the ITO bus station saw this and immediately shooed him away. I knew the puppy was only targeting students from SPA. After this incident, I became very cautious and ignored him, so that he would not follow me.

My SPA days would be incomplete without mentioning the plants and trees there. What amazed me most upon arriving for my interview were the many *Cassia fistula* trees that adorned its campus. Next to the balcony of my hostel room stood a milkweed tree, which, when in bloom, had a sweet scent. The overgrown branches of the mulberry tree spread outside the compound wall of the college, near the out-gate. Birds and passersby alike enjoyed its fruit. Towards the end of every year, there would be a chickenpox outbreak, with one to two victims, including my neighbours. As soon as news of the spread leaked out, my friend and neighbour, Susan, would take all of us along and rush to the in-gate, near which were planted some neem trees. We would take with us bunches of leaves, and then, for one to two weeks, the bathrooms would be filled with the sharp smell of crushed neem leaves and antiseptics.

Much like the seasonal outbreaks of chickenpox, earthquakes made their presence felt every year. Although it had originated somewhere in Nepal or Afghanistan, the tremor also affected Delhi. Twice or thrice it happened when I was inside the hostel, and once when a review was going on in our second-year studio in the academic block.

I was totally afraid of Delhi's summers, which acted like an overheated oven. We would want a cooler or a fan to always follow us. I even had to bring about radical changes in my food habits, especially lunch. Avoiding spicy food, I resorted to a mixture of curd and chilli as the only 'side dish' with rice. This really helped me keep my body temperature low.

Celebrations were another thing that kept all of us close together. I could become a part of various formal and festive occasions both at our college and at the MB hostel. SPA was indeed a mini-India, with students coming from all parts of India. Some students were from other countries and regions like Bhutan, Nepal and Africa. Irrespective of our backgrounds, we celebrated everything together, and there were enough reasons and occasions for get-togethers and functions; Fresher's Days, Farewell Days, Thanks-giving party, national and regional festivals (*Onam*, *Diwali*, *Holi*, *Ganeshotsav*), New Year celebrated under different names across India (Tamil, Telugu and Bengali), SPA's own 'Utopia', and the like. The best *Onam* celebrations I have ever had in my life were the ones held in the MB hostel. In fact, everyone either had or found 'n' number of reasons, personal or otherwise, to celebrate every moment there.

Outside the life of SPA, I have seen the Durga Puja celebrations held at the Chittaranjan Park, the Eid eve at Shahjahanabad (present day Chandni Chowk and Red Fort area), *Holi* celebrations at Neelima's home, and the *Karwa Chowt* happening on the banks of Yamuna while crossing the bridge to Laxmi Nagar, singers performing *Khawali* at Nizamuddin Dargah, art exhibitions in NGMA, Lalitkala Academy, among others.

Prior to winter, nearing *Diwali*, a student-run charitable unit in SPA named 'Muskaan' would buy clothes, winter wear, blankets, art supplies, crackers, toys, and sweets to distribute to underprivileged children living on the streets of Delhi. With the Muskaan team, I visited the slum in Majnu ka Tila. I saw the dark and destitute face of Delhi, and understood the need for human compassion. It was so heart-warming to see the smiles on the faces of the kids as they received the gifts wrapped with love and care. My peers showed me that the privileged have a tremendous responsibility towards serving our fellow beings who struggle to make ends meet, kindling smiles on their faces and hope in their lives. While we celebrated *Diwali* within the confines of our college, Muskaan ensured that we also helped those living with less than the bare minimum resources celebrate at least some moments of their lives. The sky lanterns that were flown high at the MB hostel during the *Diwali* celebrations reminded me of the innocent smiles of the kids in Majnu ka Tila.

Exploring places was an integral part of life in SPA. Sometimes, being highly saturated and exhausted, the entire class fled outside Delhi, to places far away, yet reachable in one night. The first of such an escape was to Nainital, then to Lansdowne (both in Uttarakhand), next to Bhangarh in Rajasthan, and finally, to Dalhousie, Khajjiar and Chamba (all in Himachal Pradesh). And, if we knew we were about to reach the saturation point, we would make short trips within Delhi; the 'infinite' number of monuments, the majority being graves and tombs, religious centres like churches, mosques, mandirs and gurudwaras, heritage walks, several conventions and conferences, art exhibitions, musical shows, the '*Bhavan*s' of various States in India that served authentic, delicious food specific to each state—Andhra Pradesh Bhavan, Kerala House and Maharashtra Sadan, and many more.

Walking along the boulevards, I enjoyed Delhi's shade. Roaming around and shopping from its lively, way-side, local and designed markets, cheered me up. Janpath, Connaught Place, Palika Bazaar, Dilli Haat, Sarojini Nagar, Lajpath, Chandni Chowk, Majnu ka Tila and Sadar Bazaar—are all familiar to me now. India Gate and Rashtrapati Bhavan in Rajpath, Humayun's Tomb, Nizamuddin Dargah, Hauz Khas, Safdurjung's Tomb, Ferozshah Kotla, Purana Qila and Zoo, Jama Masjid and Red Fort, Lodhi Gardens, Lotus Temple, National Crafts Museum and National Museum were some of our many weekend destinations.

On my first visit to the Qutb Complex and Mehrauli, as part of our studio project, I never imagined I would become a regular visitor there. I do not even remember the number of times I had been there in those two years. The integrated (interdisciplinary) studio, which comprised Master's students from four different streams, including ours, also conducted studies on the Mehrauli Archaeological Park. Groups got regrouped again, and I joined Sudipta for the documentation and study of Madhi Masjid in Mehrauli. Thus, I used to frequent Mehrauli, a place where I spent most of my first semester looking for clues on its physical and non-physical aspects and extracting the meanings of those traces and ruins.

Monuments of Delhi tell many stories: their conceptualization, construction, and also the chronicles of their existence to this 21st century. They convey various emotions. Some speak of valour, strength, superiority and technological excellence, while others speak of love, affection and association. A few possess stories tracing back to the time of epics, while a few others are in their infancy. Some have been cherished for generations, while others have been left in ruins only to fade out quietly.

There were moments when we felt proud of being Indian. I find it my privilege to have seen the Republic Day Parade in 2015. Because of the location in a prime institutional area, SPA would be closed either during the forenoon or the afternoon sessions, a few days prior to the Parade Day, for rehearsals and preparations to be done. On 26th January 2015, we left the hostel early in the morning, took the metro, walked more than a kilometre, and finally, after many security checks, we took our respective seats in the gallery. It started raining, and I shivered in the freezing winter. Disregarding the plays of climate, we kept our focus only on the Rajpath, taking pride as citizens of India. The 50th anniversary celebration of the 1965 Indo-Pak war was also hosted at Rajpath. Though I have been against any sort of war, the exhibition gave me a brief idea of the sophisticated defence systems of India that have long been protecting us, which I had not known earlier. We also took part in the Independence Day celebrations in Central Park. I have been to the Mughal Gardens in Rashtrapati Bhavan. It opens to the public once a year, offering a chance to see very rare, beautiful varieties of flowers and plants.

As part of our studio projects, we went outside Delhi as well: to Varanasi and Shillong. For the ICLAFI International Conference in 2015, we landed at Bhopal, and for the internship, I spent two months in Chennai, Thanjavur, and Alleppey. I had to leave Delhi during the site visits for my thesis as well. Amidst our studies in Varanasi, I was notified that I had won an award for my entry to the 'Meragra' Design Competition. Getting permission from the college, I went to Agra, accompanied by one of my classmates, Sreejith. Left with a day, we had to convince the station master to get train tickets. I told him I had to attend the ceremony at the Taj Mahal, in Agra, in which the chief guest would be the then Uttar Pradesh Chief Minister, Shri. Akhilesh Yadav. Knowing this, he felt happy and issued us the emergency tickets. The next morning, even in the intense sun, I could look at the Taj. The white marble monument seemed enveloped by and suspended from the moving clouds in the sky. While handing over the special mention to me, the CM asked where I was from. I replied, "From Kerala". He announced it through the mic at once. Another moment of pride!

Over my two years in Delhi, I learnt so much, albeit gradually. I learnt to love myself, and find beauty and joy in anything and everything that I sensed, thought and did. Getting together with people and places became easier. I started travelling to far-off places unplanned, both alone and with others. I tweaked my food habits while keeping myself healthy. My aversion to street food slowly eroded, and I started eating it. I have even started eating non-vegetarian food from outside. I learnt to wash my clothes every day, which became easier than ever. During winter, I could wash my clothes even when hot water was not available. On the day we came back to the hostel after our studies in Shillong, I washed all my clothes that very night. The rainy days in Shillong were unfavourable for drying clothes, which was why I had to bring all my soiled clothes to Delhi. Through better management of time and space, I created my own world even in a chaotic and congested space. Having witnessed and withstood various terrors and tremors, I grew stronger. It was no more difficult for me to balance my studies and the many moments of fun and fright. And I loved working day and night, fighting all odds. The late-night group work in my classmates' rooms, the prolonged wait in front of the printer for the A0 sheets—all turned out to be great, insignificant moments of happiness.

In order to adapt to changes in life, I learnt to use the two life-changing words judiciously: 'yes' to certain things which I had so far refused to do, and 'no' to certain things which I had nodded to till then. I was taught so many lessons as well. I could accomplish all these tasks with the constant love and support extended by my dear friends and brilliant teachers, to whom I will be indebted for a lifetime. Delhi opened my eyes and mind, and helped me rediscover myself.

I was slowly acclimatizing to the environs of Delhi before being transplanted to my homeland. The thoughts about the time spent in Delhi and the feeling of leaving the place forever disturbed me a lot. During the last days in Delhi, there was heavy rain and storm outside, and heartbreaking pain and strain inside.

However, I arrived at my home with a refreshed and open mind, ready to receive all the goodness of life. As days passed, my memories of SPA and my dear friends distressed me a lot. What I missed the most were the days of celebration of solidarity and togetherness. I missed the birthday bash done at midnight, with cakes being ordered late night; the countless loops we walked inside the campus; fun chats with senior students, classmates and juniors of all streams; outings in auto, rickshaws and metro, through Delhi's veins to the many monuments, cultural centres, malls, markets, restaurants, theatres, and places of worship. The unmatched unity among students was beyond any barriers of language, nativity, or culture.

One year just flew by, devoid of any fun. In the freezing winter of January 2017, Delhi called me back, once again, to gift me something special and to share that joy with me. On 19th January, hearing my name being called at the Siri Fort Auditorium, I moved towards the dais and received my Gold Medal for the Masters in Architectural Conservation 2014-16, and I could see my parents witness that proud moment. The following day, in the drizzling, frigid evening, I went with Sneha to one of my favourite places in Delhi, Rajpath, which was gearing up for another Republic Day.

11 DILLI HAAT AND NATIONAL CRAFTS MUSEUM

Like poles repel, and opposite poles attract each other. My Master's classmate Sudipta and I belonged to the latter group. We were entirely distinct from one another. Yet, the bond of friendship between us was far beyond what words could describe. There were some places in Delhi that we had been to together, which eventually became our favourite hangout spots. Two such places were Dilli Haat in INA and the National Crafts Museum in Pragati Maidan. As an ardent promoter of handicrafts, she introduced me to both.

Almost every weekend, we used to go to Mehrauli as part of our first-semester studio project. As the visits became more frequent, I quickly learned the routes and modes of transport that took us there. I would walk all the way to Pragati Maidan metro station and take the metro to Rajiv Chowk, our meeting place. Since she was not staying in the hostel that semester, we always had to decide on our meeting place. Then we would both rush to the yellow line and catch the metro to Qutb Minar. The rest of our journey was by auto-rickshaws. After finishing our site studies and documentation, we would head to INA on the yellow line. Dilli Haat is within walking distance, just next to the INA metro station.

After collecting our tickets at the entrance, we would proceed to the stalls. The first impression I had was that of an Indian village with *chowk*s and markets where people would gather and interact, and artisans would sell their locally produced artistic works and crafts.

*Haat*s are weekly markets, and the traditional ones were mobile in nature. Consistency and continuity in services are key to catering to Delhi's multicultural urban population. Dilli Haat aims to bridge the gap between the traditional rural *haat*s and contemporary urban needs. This is achieved by bringing together a multitude of crafts, cuisine, and cultural activities from different regions of India, permanently under one umbrella.

A diverse range of India's incredible arts and crafts can be found there in their authentic forms. Handlooms, silks, various embroideries, handicrafts, musical instruments and toys, folk arts, pottery, ceramics, wooden works, and much more—in different colours, tones, hues, vibrancy and textures—were sold in those stalls. In some stalls, sellers would sit on the floor and market their products, restoring a personal connection between artisan and buyer that was lost in the impersonal environment of virtual shopping and modern malls promoting mass-produced goods. It creates a win-win situation: buyers can enjoy hands-on shopping alongside other cultural activities, while artisans gain a wider clientele for their region-specific and handmade products. The surrounding views offered a feast for the eyes.

My companion has a profound interest in and great respect for arts and crafts. She would take me to stalls and souvenir shops selling unique products and help me choose the right ones. I was really surprised when she made an observation about me: "Jessin, you are very choosy". And that holds true; I still spend a lot of time deliberating over choices, sometimes even hours.

Moving ahead of the stalls, one might please one's taste buds at the food courts, which serve ethnic cuisine and local foods belonging to various States and Union Territories of India. Some remained closed on all our visits, but the one from Sikkim was an exception, as it always remained open. We would both have our *momo*s and *thupka* (noodles served in a hot broth). Sudipta, owing to her deep interest in the arts, was also interested in the products and cuisine of the East and Northeast of India. I presume it might be due to her roots in Bengal.

At the end of the trail, an open stage might host performances, where we would spend some time enjoying the shows.

The texture of the stone pavements, the exposed brickwork of the buildings, thoughtful landscaping, the interplay of level differences; the crowd that respects the fine craftsmanship of artists and artisans; the quietness of the place which was always given a musical rendering by the sound of the winds that seeped through the alleys and the courts, and of the chimes and beads hanging from the eaves of the stalls; the myriad colours used in the handicrafts; the mirror work in some, reflecting the panoramic views and the lighting around; the raw and rustic aroma of the handmade products and the scent of local delicacies wafting through the air; all contribute to the sense of place there—an 'urban haat island'.

After saying goodbye to Dilli Haat late in the evening, we would catch the metro to Rajiv Chowk, where we would say good night and go our separate ways.

Another favourite spot of ours was the National Crafts Museum in Pragati Maidan, designed by architect Charles Correa. The National Crafts Museum and Hastkala Academy, as it is officially called, features a multitude of arts and crafts, such as textiles, paintings, and puppets. There are galleries displaying textiles, cultic crafts featuring ritualistic objects, courtly crafts, sculptures, metal works, crafts in wood, folk art, and so on. Here, one could interact with the exhibits and feel enlivened by their charm, unlike in more clinical museums that offer little room for dialogue and seem to present exhibits without life or vigour.

Much like Dilli Haat, one can find a 'mini India' in the unique artistic and architectural treasures displayed in the National Crafts Museum. The essence of Indian villages is recreated here through several distinct open spaces and the incorporation of many tangible and intangible heritage elements.

Craftsmen and artisans could be seen working on intricate designs at various stages of their specialized craft. Though they could sell their artworks to visitors, they showed no trace of commercial greed. They valued their art above any returns they might gain by selling it. As soon as they sold a product, they would get back to their creative process, which has been an integral part of their life and livelihood. It has become their passion and their very raison d'être.

A true and gifted artist works to fulfil his or her mind and give perfect form to his or her imagination and concept about the art at hand. Such true artists could be seen in different parts of India—to name a few: the bead artists from Jammu and Kashmir, the weavers of Benares silk and Balaramapuram handlooms. The primary goal of traditional artisans working on handicrafts is to mould their ideas rather than to make money.

Once, at Sudipta's request, an artist there cut out a bird on light yellow paper, measuring around two square inches. The precision with which he wielded his small scissors showed his deep dedication to that craft, regardless of the size of the canvas. She gave it to me, and I kept it inside my wallet against a black paper to give it a contrasting background and frame. Since then, that had been its permanent place, and I could revisit those memories every time I opened my wallet.

The museum also displays India's architectural heritage interactively by recreating those spaces. It introduces us to age-old traditions in Indian architecture, such as *jharokas* (projecting windows), internal courtyards, exquisite wooden work seen on elements like doors and pillars, *chabutras* (bird/pigeon houses), and shingles on the roof. What I found most attractive at this museum was the open-air exhibit of the village complex, which encompassed vernacular housing, courtyards, and shrines, all representative of various parts of India.

The trails through Dilli Haat and the Crafts Museum were enriching and overwhelming, as both presented to us a glimpse of the plethora of traditions and cultures in India. They differ in their outlook: the former is a market, and the latter is a museum. Yet, they share the same goal: to help preserve, develop, and enrich the invaluable art and heritage of India, passed down through generations of artists and artisans. Although both are presented in a subtle and simple manner, they have a deeper meaning and motive to convey.

The modest buildings in both Dilli Haat and Crafts Museum recede into the background to highlight the skills of Indian art and heritage. Because of the smaller building footprints in both, they are an ideal choice for people seeking walkable open spaces in Delhi's urban setting. The humility of the various built and unbuilt elements provides peace of mind and happiness while experiencing both ensembles. Their simple but clear presentation offers a grand treat and a great retreat, with India's diversity being served on the same platter—the essence of Indianness!

12 AN ESCAPE TO NAINITAL

It was a genuine struggle to get through the reviews of my first-year studio in M.Arch. After one such review, exhaustion overwhelmed everyone in our class. We desperately needed a sanctuary to disappear into, one where none of us could be traced for that weekend. Someone suggested Nainital, a hill station in Uttarakhand, just a night's travel from New Delhi. We chose it as our destination, as none of us had been there before. The winter in Delhi was at the doorstep. So we wrapped ourselves in winter clothes as it was a trip planned to the mountainous terrain located further north, which would have already embraced winter.

Late in the evening, we started off from the Anand Vihar bus terminal. The darkness outside and the fatigue after a tiring day did not let me enjoy the scenic trip uphill. Early in the morning, we reached the Himalayan town of Nainital. The picturesque view of the small hill town, around a lake, studded by mountains all around, was breathtakingly beautiful, leaving me spellbound. There were no signs of snow during our visit, as it was too early to find it.

Nainital is located in the Kumaon foothills of the outer Himalayas. It sits in a valley around the eye-shaped lake named

Naini. As with most places in India, Nainital also has its roots in mythology, linked to Goddess Sati. It is believed that Naini Lake is one of the 51 *Shakti Peeth*s, the sacred sites marked by the falling of Sati's body parts on earth. The spot where her right eye fell became the "lake of the eye". Thus the name Nainital—"*Nain*" meaning eye and "*tal*" meaning lake in Hindi. The goddess is still worshipped at the Naina Devi Temple today.

The Naini Lake aligns with the northwest-southeast axis, curving inwards to the west. Tree-populated mountains stand on the western side of the lake. They appeared hardly touched by humans, though that was not actually the case. The eastern side of the lake, even though hilly, was the denser zone with heavy footfall. Naina Devi Temple sits to the north of the lake.

We refreshed ourselves with tea and some snacks and strolled along the paved avenue beside the lake. It is called the Mall Road, a 1.5-kilometre-long pedestrian road, located to the east of the lake. The walk was the perfect way to rejuvenate our exhausted bodies and minds. The maple trees on both sides, climbers with flowers, the stone pavements, the way-side park benches, the chirping of birds and the chatter of the heavily clad people passing by, the cool breeze, a harbinger of the winter which was yet to intensify,.... So relieving a feeling it was. In the lake, some boats carrying people kept on rowing around, some were lying idle along the banks, and some lay here and there, abandoned and broken.

Without a second thought, we all went boating from the boat club near the Naina Devi temple. While the boat was caressing the ripples it had created in the lake, the waters were scintillating in the rays of the morning sun. Swans dabbling in the lake were a beautiful sight after sunrise that day. It became slightly warmer as the boat rowed through the centre of the lake, away from the shade of the avenue trees. My mind was getting lighter as if it were floating in the lake.

After having lunch, we set out from the lakeshore in a car to explore the places uphill. The car, panting for breath and sweating, took us to several designated viewpoints uphill, which made sightseeing easier and effortless. The views we discover for ourselves might be better than those designated as popular merely for the sake of convenience. There might be numerous such viewpoints lying undiscovered in Nainital, like hidden gems. However, time constraints limited us to the designated ones. Once we reached the top, we found a rocky outcrop overlooking the valley, where the clouds would come down to greet us. The view was so immersive that we did not notice time running out. Carrying us, our car sped downhill towards the lakeshore.

People were flocking to the lakeshore as the sun started setting. Wayside businesses and evening markets were abuzz with people. That is where I did my winter shopping that year. Enjoying the activities around, we headed towards the Naina Devi temple. The temple premises had become crowded in the evening. We stayed away from the crowd and sat on a parapet nearby. The views from there were so stunning, and the temple seemed to be the focus of the entire town. Perhaps that was the liveliest of all the locations I had seen in Nainital, and the best viewpoint as well. The lake was still busy with boats and people.

The extra time left helped us visit St. Francis Church, located towards the southeast of the town. The churches in hill towns would look similar on account of various determinants, such as the local climate, the availability of wood and stone, and the influence of Western architecture. As it was getting late and cold, we decided to leave. The town was colourfully lit while we retraced our steps along the avenue to the bus station.

I found the night view of Nainital even better than the day's. And to me, that is the same for any hill town or rugged mountainous landscape. The lake, hills, trees, buildings and silhouettes of people—everything just merged seamlessly into that darkness, contiguous with the night sky. Lights of various colours and intensities pierced the darkness around, while the sky was powdered with stars. It was the density and similarity of the illumination associated with various activities that helped me to distinguish what was what.

The buzz of birds, people, and businesses broke the silence of the streets. To ready themselves for a sound sleep, the bejewelled hills around pulled over their blankets. High-spirited and mischievous ripples in the lake were lovingly quarrelling with each other. Yet, the lake remained calm and still, reflecting, since time immemorial, the life of the town and the love for it, the lofty mountains around, and the high sky above. Each frame of the place was so captivating, like a brilliantly illustrated canvas, that I felt like escaping to Nainital, once again, unplanned.

13 THE ROCKY AND THE REVERED LANDS

I was attending the ICLAFI (International Committee of Legal Administrative and Financial Issues) International Conference 2015 at the School of Planning and Architecture (SPA), Bhopal. Like the other attendees, I was looking forward to a long break between its sessions to head off-campus. And as expected, we got a full day off to explore the city. As a river splits into its distributaries, the members got split into various groups, according to the places they wished to go to. I was part of a group of five that decided to go to Bhimbetka and Sanchi, each at a distance of around 60 kilometres to the southeast and northeast, respectively, from SPA, the conference venue.

To hire a vehicle, we had to travel into the city, about 20 kilometres away. Even though there were a lot of green spaces in the city, they seemed minuscule in the backdrop of the abundant heat and dust. Putting an end to the long wait of about an hour, a car came to take us to our destination.

As we drove toward the countryside, trees and plants emerged one by one, bringing lush greenery into the scene. The mountainous trail to the Bhimbetka rock shelters, located inside the Ratapani Wildlife Sanctuary in the foothills of the Vindhya ranges, showcased the beauty of lush greenery with patches of rocks dispersed here and there. We alighted from the car and followed the sloped pathway leading to the hilltop. The archaeological site with rocky outcrops seemed ordinary at first glance.

The extraordinary aspects of the site, as old as the Stone Age, and its outstanding universal value, which led to its inscription as a UNESCO World Heritage Site, were to be unveiled shortly.

As we proceeded further uphill, the wonders hidden in Bhimbetka were revealed one by one. The hilltop was dotted with many natural caves formed out of sandstone. There are over 700 rock shelters in that area. Among the 243 caves found in Bhimbetka, only a few, numbering 15, were open to the public. The caves are numbered to assist visitors with navigation throughout the site. Once we go near them, the 'mysteries' of the site unfurl. What had been awaiting us was an exhibition of paintings by 'unknown prehistoric artists' on the natural canvases of rock masses, set atop the hill amidst a thick forest.

The caves and rock shelters, formed out of huge rock pieces, bear vivid expressions of artworks that date back as early as the Stone Age. However, the paintings were discovered only in the mid-20th century. They were done on the walls of the caves and on the high ceilings underneath the rock pieces serving as roofs. With the limited natural resources available then, the prehistoric dwellers beautifully portrayed the life of their times on the rock surfaces. The cave paintings in natural hues of green, red, white, brown, and black, depicting themes like human figures, dancers, animals, hunters with their weapons and prey, and warriors on horseback, still look fresh and vibrant. The rock-art narrates the emotions our ancestors experienced while living secluded in and sheltered by the caves, defending against the attacks of wild animals and natural forces. They had recorded their joyous moments during celebrations, their livelihood as hunter-gatherers, and the fight with the wild for survival, among others.

Life-sized models of people demonstrate the life within this settlement in those times and show how the artists made paintings on the rock surfaces. Apart from the cave paintings, archaeological studies and excavations in the caves and other areas around them have brought to light the artefacts used by the occupants, including stone tools. In an era when human existence was a struggle against the wilderness and the unknown, these people settled here, finding the time to brilliantly express their creative imaginations on an enduring canvas. The hardships of a rough and uneasy life were so excellently portrayed on the cave walls through their gifted artistic hands.

The site had continuous habitation, belonging to different prehistoric periods—including the Upper Paleolithic Period (Old Stone Age), the Mesolithic Period (Middle Stone Age) and the Chalcolithic Period (early Bronze Age)—as well as the early historic period. Thus, the paintings found in these natural rock shelters tell a layered history. The artistic works of successive periods in the historical timeline record the cultural evolution of humans over time: hunter-gatherers leading a nomadic lifestyle; cultivators leading a settled life; and the early concepts of religion and spirituality. The canvas chosen to depict their hardships and happiness was rougher, more durable, and well beyond the reach of vandals, who might otherwise have defaced them with worthless graffiti.

What really makes these cave paintings distinct and distinguished is the fact that they give evidence of prehistoric life thousands of years before scripts and inscriptions appeared for the first time in the region. It took several millennia for the first civilization to appear in the Indian subcontinent, in the valley of the Indus River and its tributaries. It was quite surprising for me to know that some humans leading a nomadic lifestyle in nature-granted shelters had created wonders with surpassing artistic skills. They show that art is an outcome of a free and creative mind that need not be that of a civilized mind. Be it the walls of caves or of buildings, man has always found a canvas to articulate or express the artist inside. The prehistoric paintings of the primitive hunter-gatherers, and the frescoes and murals of much later periods by the civilized lot, testify to this.

It was amazing to learn that there were artists among prehistoric humans. In my observation, artists nowadays mostly belong to two broad categories. One is a full-time artist who views art as an inseparable part of life and creates artwork for the pleasure of the mind or for a livelihood. The other is a part-time artist who views art as a hobby and creates artworks during their leisure time for relief from various sorts of pressure. Whether there were designated artists among the settlers who were assigned to paint the caves, or all the settlers contributed to the paintings, is an unresolved question in Bhimbetka.

Anyway, those artists could never have imagined that their 'open art gallery' with paintings using linear representation, geometric figures, and natural pigments would outlive the generations to come, or that it would become curious subjects for art critics and historians, or that their work possessed such outstanding universal value that it would be inscribed on the World Heritage List conceptualized and instituted by the humans of the 20th century. While I was lost in such thoughts, it drizzled.

Very soon, we departed for Sanchi, which lies 90 kilometres to the north of the Bhimbetka rock shelters. On the way, our group was joined by three more people, and one left us midway for another destination. We passed through the location of the gas tragedy that had left its black mark in Bhopal's history, where nothing much was left to see, except ruins. After all, a disaster leaves behind few material belongings; only the tragic memories and trauma are etched into eternity.

During our journey, we could also cross the Tropic of Cancer. This 23.5 degree latitude that lies to the north of the Equator denotes the northernmost latitude where the sun is seen directly overhead. It passes through eight states in India and falls in the city of Bhopal as well. The name-board and the oblique broken lines marked across the road help to locate it on the ground. It is through these sorts of simple, tangible elements that a layperson gets to know the otherwise intangible yet significant geographic characteristics and contexts associated with a place.

In the distant horizon to our right, a few stupas slowly started appearing on the mountainous terrain of Sanchi. The humble entry to the site, the road that takes us to the hilltop, the way the monuments appeared one by one in the distance, all reminded me of my trail to the Bhimbetka rock shelters. Sanchi is a prime sacred location related to Buddhism. It has several stupas atop a sandstone hill and on its slopes. *Vihara*s, which housed the Buddhist monks in the monastery, and temples of different periods, including those of the Guptas, are also found within the complex.

A stupa is an important form of Buddhist architecture. However, the concept behind it predates Buddhism. It was inspired by the burial mounds built to bury great teachers and the mounds built over the ashes of tribal chiefs of the Vedic period. The Buddhist stupa houses the relics (sacred remains) and ashes of the Buddha. Under the patronage of the Mauryan emperor Asoka, who was the first king to embrace Buddhism, the earth and rubble structure of the stupa got a dignified form. The Great Stupa is the largest of all the stupas in Sanchi. It was originally built by Asoka in the 3rd Century BCE and enlarged under the Shungas in the 1st Century BCE. I felt so happy to see and touch the monument built about two millennia ago by an emperor who ruled over most of what is India today. Timelessness is a quality of architectural masterpieces. Besides the written and oral pieces of information, architecture helps rulers and commoners echo the saga of their golden period to the generations to come.

Like any ancient monument, the design and form of a stupa also have symbolic associations and meanings. The final geometrical form of a stupa, based on a circle, symbolizes the 'wheel of law' (*dharma chakra*). Also, a circular geometry was found ideal to perform the Buddhist ritual of endless circumambulation around Buddha's sacred relics, which helps in understanding the four 'Noble Truths' taught by the Buddha. The hemispherical dome symbolizes the *anda* (egg) or womb containing the sacred relics of the Buddha. Four profusely carved *torana*s (entry gateways) that open up the *vedika* (sacred railing) from four cardinal directions provide entry to the Great Stupa. Circumambulatory pathways called *pradakshinapatha* could be seen both on the ground and on the upper levels, the latter of which is accessed via a double staircase to the south. The hemispherical mound is crowned by the *chhatra* (a three-tiered umbrella) enclosed by the *harmika* (a square-shaped railing). They symbolize the Bodhi tree surrounded by the sacred *vedika.*

While sensing the Great Stupa of Sanchi in its three-dimensional form, I recollected having made its sketch in the History of Architecture sketchbook during my bachelor's. A stupa, as understood by me, is the focal point where enlightenment has been entombed; a spot of immense energy and spiritual resonance stored within. The Buddhist architectural theory was discussed in great depth in the lectures of our beloved Professor at SPA, New Delhi, Late Ar. Vikram Lall, who had done extensive research on the same.

I visited the Dhamek Stupa at Sarnath a few months ago. The form of it was quite different from those seen at Sanchi. Though their forms may vary, the idea behind this solid structure remains the same, which is to practice endless circumambulation around the sacred objects that it encloses.

Stupas were thought to be mounds built above treasures, tempting treasure hunters to break them apart. Having discovered that the stupas contained only Buddha's relics, they left them. Later, it took very meticulous efforts to restore and eventually conserve them. The archaeological surveys conducted by the British in India have had their benefits too. Those explorations helped bring to light the existence of a rich and diverse heritage in India, which remained unknown to many till their discovery and scientific documentation.

Some worshippers clad in pink-coloured dresses could be seen circumambulating the Great Stupa along its elevated *pradakshinapatha*. In our train journey from New Delhi to Bhopal, I saw several devotees from Sri Lanka wearing the same pink-coloured dresses. Walking along the elevated *pradakshinapatha*, I looked around; the stupas and other structures on the hilltop and slopes, farmlands and fields in the nearby valley, the low and broader mountains afar, and the blue sky slowly switching to warm colours signalling the setting of the Sun. Heading back to Bhopal, the stupas slowly disappeared from my eyes.

The UNESCO World Heritage Sites of the Rock Shelters of Bhimbetka and the Buddhist monuments at Sanchi, with extremely different characters, convey different levels and meanings of life. Bhimbetka represented a life of pure existence driven by biological needs, wherein humanity continually strove to resolve its conflict with nature and to tame it, while the concept of God remained in its primitive stages. Sanchi, in contrast, was established by a religious group seeking enlightenment, driven by theological principles, wherein the relationship between humanity, the world, and God—and the search for the knowledge to attain peace and happiness—were explored, and wherein one strove to resolve the conflict with their own thoughts and deeds.

On our way back to the city, we got out of the car and captured a memory in which all seven of us held our hands together and lined up beside the Tropic of Cancer. And we continued the journey, building layers of much treasured memories.

14 THE WEAVERS OF TRAVANCORE

Living beings spend day and night building their basic need of shelter with intricacy, precision, and perfection; a weaver bird building its nest, bees building their hive, an architect designing a beautiful home, and the like. The basic need for clothing is not dissimilar. A fabric is made in different ways, like weaving, knitting, and the production of non-woven fabrics.

Of the many clothes I have seen so far, the ones worn during *Onam*, such as the *mundu* (*dhoti*) and saris, in their off-white coloured fabric with a multitude of designs and coloured borders, have always fascinated me. *Dhoti*s have been a common sight for me, as my father wears them paired with shirts on almost every occasion, official or casual, unless he is travelling out of the state or abroad. Wearing dhotis made him stand out from his male colleagues, who preferred trousers to *dhoti*s. Thus, since a very young age, I have been curious to know the story behind them. Cotton fibres are woven to create *dhoti*s. My father prefers cotton dhotis woven on handlooms, which are more comfortable, durable, and costlier than the ones made on power looms. During our informal discussions, he had mentioned one of their places of origin, Balaramapuram, a town that lies on the outskirts of Thiruvananthapuram city.

It was mere happenstance that I chose *Saliyatteruvu*, in Balaramapuram, for my Master's thesis. The weavers of *Saliyatteruvu* belong to the *Saliyar* community, who have been engaged in weaving fine handloom products for over two centuries. In 1795, the then ruler of the erstwhile Travancore State, Kartika Tirunal Rama Varma, shifted the capital from Padmanabhapuram to Thiruvananthapuram. His successor, Avittom Tirunal Balaramavarma, aimed to establish a commercial and industrial town for the new capital. To achieve this, the town of 'Balaramapuram' was established in 1810, named after the ruler. He brought five occupational groups to Balaramapuram, one being the *Saliyar* weavers from Valliyur in Tamil Nadu.

The handloom products by *Saliyar* weavers were initially designed for the royals of Travancore, inspired by royal patronage. In the 20th century, they began meeting the needs of the common people as well. The town flourished immensely in a brief spell of time, with the fame of its handloom products reaching even overseas, under the brand name 'Balaramapuram'. The handicraft, officially named 'Balaramapuram Saris and Fine Cotton Fabrics', has received the Geographic Indication tagging since 2009.

As time elapsed, symptoms of decline started to appear in this historic town as well, which had witnessed all three stages in its life cycle: founding, flourishing, and falling. The traditional handloom industry, passed down through generations of *Saliyar*s in the *Saliyatteruvu*, started its phase of downfall due to several reasons. They include the introduction of power loom products that are comparatively cheaper, spatial and financial issues, labour issues, lack of royal patronage, the rise of middlemen, and so on. Even though products branded as 'Balaramapuram handlooms' are being sold in the market woven by both *Saliyar* and non-*Saliyar* weavers in and around Balaramapuram, the traditional products from *Saliyatteruvu* have been slowly disappearing from the mainstream.

I spent twenty days in *Saliyatteruvu*, though intermittently, about ten years ago. It helped me forge a close bond with the place, the people, and the more-than-two-century-old practices of weaving followed there. There were around 400 households with over 1500 residents. The settlement houses *Saliyar*s, and other communities that have been providing various services to them, like *Brahmin*s (priests), *Vannan* (washer-men), and *Nassuvan* (barbers). During my study, most of the *Saliyar* households had weaving and associated activities as a livelihood. Other than labourers hired to work at homes, the members of the households themselves contributed to the home-based industry, thus becoming a part of the labour market. I could recognize each one of them, by their names, family, kith and kin, the jobs they did, the location of their houses in the settlement and the stage(s) of weaving they were involved in, akin to an aspiring sociologist. I became a mutual friend of all the residents there, and at some point, I found myself at one with them.

Many good people, in several ways, had helped me with my studies there. Apart from the vital inputs that enriched my knowledge base, they also provided me with food and drink, and I accepted all of them wholeheartedly. The young Saravanan, who knew the settlement, assisted me in my surveys, introducing me to his neighbours. *Amma*—as I used to call her lovingly—was an old woman in her mid-60s then who provided me with lunch on almost all days. She used to prepare my favourite dishes for lunch and would stock snacks I liked the most to give me on my way back home. She would serve me lunch and continue talking to her peers from her neighbourhood. After lunch, we would both watch her favourite Tamil TV serials together. When it came to the legacy of weaving, she took pride in the designs she had woven in her youth, like handloom fabrics featuring lotus motifs and other floral patterns.

Most of the residents spoke to me in Malayalam, mixed with a Tamil accent. However, within their community, they conversed in Tamil. Sometimes, I too communicated with them in Tamil. Initially, while doing my surveys, I struggled to understand their weaving terminology, but I soon overcame this hurdle. As I started communicating with them in their language of speaking and weaving, it made my job easier, and theirs as well.

It takes several days to finish a handloom product, as it has to pass through a number of hands before it finally reaches the customer. The assembly-line production adopted by 20th century industrialists can be seen in its traditional form in the handloom weaving practiced in *Saliyatteruvu* for over two centuries. Fine quality cotton and coloured yarn, and zari are the raw materials to be procured. The yarn is cured in water in open tanks built in the rear yards of houses or near the public wells in the streets. Once cured, it is washed and taken for winding on a charka. Then comes warping, which needs a wooden drum and a creel. The activities of winding and warping are mostly done by ladies while handling their daily household chores. Sizing, once done on the streets, has been moved out of *Saliyatteruvu* due to space constraints. After sizing, the process of beaming rolls the warp. The weaver's beam is then mounted on a pit loom, kept within the home or in sheds outside, and the weaver gets inside the pit for weaving. Nowadays, weaving also depends on looms with elevated seats, on which a weaver can sit without having to descend into a pit. The last and final activity is quality checking and packing. After this, the finished product is taken for display in a shop or sold directly to the customer who had commissioned it. The activities seen in different stages of weaving have permeated deep into the lives of every *Saliyar*, because of which they have been able to achieve work-life balance.

Machine-made clothes are produced by power looms in bulk

quantities. Being mass-produced, they lack any affection or emotion attached to them. In contrast, handloom products are woven on handlooms operated by human hands. They are crafted one at a time with love, extreme care, and utmost patience to bring forth products of the finest attainable quality. A 90-year-old master-weaver of *Saliyatteruvu* told me he had seen the Maharaja of Travancore wearing the dhoti woven by him on the day of '*Aarattu*', the royal procession to the Shankhumukham beach. Out of curiosity, my father asked him, "How could you be so sure that you wove it?" He smiled and replied, "Wouldn't we all recognize our own children?" The hand-woven clothes look elegant and feel comfortable upon wearing. They result from the prayers, dedication, and hard work of a weaver, who invests a lifetime of skill, time, and energy into every piece.

The traditional weaving of *Saliyar*s relied heavily on the architectural aspects of the settlement. It was disheartening to see haphazard transformations in the built heritage, which have become a major cause of the decline in weaving. Each and every space in the original fabric of *Saliyatteruvu* was designed to accommodate the processes in weaving; the verandahs that open to the streets, hall, courtyard, kitchen, attic, and rear yard—all were part and parcel of the works and rituals associated with weaving. The streets were also part of the story of weaving in *Saliyatteruvu*. The process of sizing used to happen either on both sides of the street or along its middle, depending on the width of the street. Thus, it is nearly impossible to separate weaving from living in their row-houses and streets.

On every street, at any time, one could find people walking or cycling from one place to another, transporting yarn at various stages of processing. It is their hereditary occupation that still maintains the warm relationship with their neighbours and relatives, and vice versa. To keep the industry alive and their ties intact, they have been trying not to deviate from or disturb the two-century-old chain in the system of weaving. Healthy coordination and harmony in the interconnectedness of various factors have been the lifeblood of the weaving industry of *Saliyatteruvu.* It resembles the way the longer vertical threads, called warp, and the shorter horizontal threads, called weft, are interlaced upon weaving in handlooms.

The *Saliyar*s, in general, are kind-hearted, patient, hard-working and sincere; the essential qualities a weaver keeps so dear to heart. While I was doing my surveys, one resident asked me, "Aren't you afraid to walk along our streets and visit our homes, all alone?" Smilingly, I said, "No, nothing to fear at all; this is a safe and secure environment". The complex network of linkages is truly the backbone of the sustenance of *Saliyatteruvu*; the row-houses sharing common walls, the *Saliyar* community living cohesively in the different *teru*s (streets) with ties of kinship and bonds of marriage, the linkages in the workflow that keep the system of weaving going, and the like. Everyone has been working in close liaison with each other. The other four communities brought by the ruler settled in close proximity to *Saliyatteruvu.* In one way or another, they had also been involved in weaving, assisting the *Saliyar*s. Now, this inter-community linkage had been severed, as weaving started witnessing its state of decline.

I stepped into the home of a *dhoti*-seller who used to sell dhotis from *Saliyatteruvu* to offices in Thiruvananthapuram city. He said that he had been to my father's office too, and he was right, as my father used to bring home the products sold by *dhoti*-sellers in his office. I was heartened to learn that my father had been a constant supporter of and contributor to the handloom industry of *Saliyatteruvu.* I recollect purchasing handloom *dhoti*s with my family from a shop that sold handloom products in the city. While interviewing the same nonagenarian master-weaver in *Saliyatteruvu*, I came to know that the people associated with this shop once used to be the middlemen in the handloom industry, acting as vital links between the *Saliyar* weavers and the Travancore Palace.

I visited a weaving centre on a street in *Saliyatteruvu.* A few women labourers were working in pit looms. Once the interview with them concluded, one of them asked me, "Would you like to try weaving in this?" I nodded, and in no time, descended into the pit. I struggled to move the loom even an inch, quickly burning through my energy. I realized that it requires a healthy mind and a healthy body to weave using a pit loom. In a pit loom, the weavers get half-immersed in the pit; their hands and legs should move simultaneously, and their eyes should coordinate with their limbs. Over time, their minds and bodies adapt to the rhythm of their work. Half-immersed in the pit for their entire lifetime, they have been weaving unconditionally; intertwining the warp and weft of their lives and livelihoods, and their hopes and dreams.

15 STATIONING AT THE HILLS

Everyone put forth their suggestions for the final class trip, a grand escape from Delhi's blazing summer. Also, a break was imperative to relieve the stress accumulated during the final semester of my Master's. Options and opinions varied, and no consensus could be reached regarding the destinations or the number of members willing to join. The plan collapsed before its inception, even after trying so many permutations and combinations. At night, while I was watching a movie, an informal meeting took place in my hostel room to rethink the trip. That too failed, as members dropped out due to various reasons.

Only three people, including me, remained for the two-day trip planned for Chamba, Khajjiar and Dalhousie. These are all hill stations within the administrative bounds of the Chamba district of Himachal Pradesh. I firmly stood by my decision to go, as I wanted to leave Delhi with a fresh, peaceful mind after writing the final exam near the end of the semester. And the three of us decided to head northwards. I packed my bag with only the essentials, to keep it really light. After dinner, while leaving for the Anand Vihar Bus Terminal, two more from my class followed and joined us; thus, five of us set out on the journey.

While waiting for the bus, a passenger at the bus terminal fought with and attacked the person behind the barred ticket counter. The police came and solved the issue right on the spot. Our bus arrived, and quickly we got into it, without having to witness any more ruckus that might spoil our dream trip. All of us smiled at each other and shared buttermilk and snacks that were in stock.

The long hours spent on the bus overnight were tiring. However, the day dawned to pleasant, fresh sights. The trip became interesting as I enjoyed journeying through the heart of many remote areas. I could see the Bhakra Dam, a vast structure built across the Sutlej, and the Gobind Sagar Lake (or Reservoir) formed by the dam. Dedicating the Bhakra Dam to the nation, Pandit Jawaharlal Nehru, the first Prime Minister of India, had described it as the 'new temple of resurgent India' and 'the symbol of India's progress'.

Soaking up the scenic rural tracts viewed through a series of rectangular windows on the bus in transit, we had completely lost track of time. At around 10 AM, everyone sensed something was wrong with our course of travel. We were uncertain whether we were taking the right route or not, as we should have reached Chamba in the morning itself. On enquiring with the conductor about the delay, he said that we had taken the wrong bus, which would reach there only by evening. Cursing ourselves, we got off at the next station. Fortunately, there was still scope for a swap, so we moved Dalhousie forward in the itinerary and postponed Chamba.

In another bus, we reached Pathankot and had our lunch from a dhaba there. Awaiting any generous vehicle that might take us to Dalhousie, we sat on a milestone and some fallen trees lying alongside the road, like the bogies of a train. Finally ending our wait, a minibus appeared in front of us. It was terribly packed with passengers and goods. There was hardly any room to step inside. Anyhow, we managed to make space in that little ark by lifting one leg up like storks and sometimes hanging on to handgrips like monkeys. The journey progressed, so did the heat, and the bus resembled a furnace.

Thankfully, we reached Dalhousie in the afternoon. The remarkable change here, compared to the places we had been seeing, was the climate and the landscape that became cooler, more mountainous, and heavily wooded. The British established most of the hill stations in India, as they found the plains unfriendly to acclimatize to owing to high temperatures and the risk of epidemics. Dalhousie is a hill station, established by the British in the mid-19th century, as a summer retreat for their troops and bureaucrats. It was named after Lord Dalhousie, who had served as the then-Governor-General of India. He was instrumental in modernizing and connecting India, and in laying the foundations for consolidating foreign rule in India, which eventually transitioned from Company rule to British Raj once he had left India. His authoritarianism and centralizing tendencies resulted in reformative, yet unpopular, policies. One such was the Doctrine of Lapse, which resulted in gross setbacks, fueling resentment and turmoil against British rule. He was criticized for having failed to notice the early signs of the Revolt of 1857, hailed as India's First War of Independence, which occurred after his departure from India.

We strolled through the salubrious sanctuary founded by the foreigners who wanted to escape the heat and diseases that were common in the plains. Our first agenda in Dalhousie was to find a place to stay that offered the best view of the green mountains and the valleys, at a reasonable rate. We succeeded in finding a decent hotel room that satisfied our criteria. Keeping our belongings in the hotel, we went out to absorb the hill station.

The visit being in May, the climate was pleasant, not too cold to put on heavy winter clothes. We ascended Court Road, which ended at Subhash Chowk, a busy node. From there, three roads of varying gradients—namely Subhash Chowk Road, Thandi Sadak, and Garam Sadak—diverged in different directions and altitudes. The Chowk had the statue of freedom fighter Subhash Chandra Bose, after whom it was named. The viewpoint at the Chowk overlooked the mountains and the valleys.

The St. Francis Church, on a hillock to the west of Subhash Chowk, grabbed our attention. We mounted the pathway leading to the church, which was surrounded by conifers. Being set in a favourable climate and certainly having a gardener to look after it, the garden on the church premises was beautifully manicured with an abundance of flowers, especially pink roses. There was no one inside the church, except a priest. I sat on a bench for a while and went around to see the various spaces there. It was the rose window set in the stone masonry structure that impressed me the most in this late-19th century church.

We got back to the teeming Chowk, which had by then been occupied by school children, their parents, and lots of other people. I moved towards the viewpoint, which offered unparalleled views. Unfortunately, in a competitive spirit to offer the best views and experiences to the booming tourism industry, people conveniently forgot the fragile ecology of the hilly areas, the Himalayan region in particular. If uncontrolled, it would result in chronic socio-economic and ecological consequences like slope failures, the slow disappearance of native species of flora and fauna, and the displacement of natives by commercial developers, among others. The unplanned and haphazard developments in fragile zones have intensified the damages that resulted from the devastating floods seen in recent years in Uttarakhand, another Himalayan state. And here is where the local residents, authorities, businesses, and tourists have to pitch in and work closely with each other in order to shift their focus to responsible tourism development, which offers sustainable solutions with win-win outcomes.

Dalhousie had started to shiver mildly as we set forth to Gandhi Chowk as pedestrians, covering about one and a half kilometres from Subhash Chowk. Walking along the Garam Sadak, enjoying the beauty of the landscape characterized by low and high reliefs, I breathed in some fresh mountain air, which was unavailable in New Delhi due to air pollution. After a refreshing walk, we reached Gandhi Chowk. The statue of Mahatma Gandhi was a major landmark there. The Chowk, from where four roads diverged, was surrounded by a market, a church, various shops and a gallery on one side, where several groups of people were sitting together and chatting. Some protest was going on in remembrance of a child who had gone missing a few years ago.

The St. John's Church, to the northeast of Gandhi Chowk, was the first of the churches to be built in Dalhousie in the 19th century. Though set in the midst of conifers, it sits on comparatively flatter land, allowing visitors to navigate the perimeter without encountering steep changes in elevation. It had so many roses at its apsidal end. After seeing the exterior, I moved inside, where I listened to a family of parents and two kids singing devotional songs, sitting in the row across mine, on the other side of the aisle.

Leaving the church, we headed to the Mall Road, which was a lively commercial centre with heavy footfall. The Mall Road Gandhi Chowk Market is a bustling marketplace located to the south of Gandhi Chowk, where one can shop and eat while walking along the street. The sloping roofs of the Colonial-era buildings on the Mall Road stood out against the skyline, harmonizing with the conical tops of the conifers.

A mall means a sheltered promenade for leisure walks or a shopping area where traffic is excluded. Mall Roads were introduced in India in the 18th century as military residential areas, and Mall meant 'Married Accommodation and Living Line'

Road. Mall Roads have been an integral part of most of the hill stations established by the British in India. They are seen in hill stations of Himachal Pradesh, Uttarakhand, West Bengal, Sikkim, and so on. These roads are favourite spots in hill stations, thronged by businesses and tourists alike. I remember walking along the Mall Road in Nainital, to the east of Naini Lake. And one could also find the Thandi Sadak of Nainital, lining the western edge of the lake. Dalhousie was getting dark, and the coniferous trees, with their thick trunks and droopy, drowsy, evergreen foliage, made it look even darker. We went back to the hotel after a delicious dinner.

The next day, I had a refreshing start with a morning walk in the serene landscape. I walked along a road diverging from Subhash Chowk, towards a school near St. Francis Church. The sky could hardly be seen amidst the lofty conifers. As I moved a little further, the trees allowed me a clear view of a distant land, which was so fascinating to look at. Afar, beyond the green mountains, could be seen the snow-capped peaks of the Himalayas. Those peaks seemed to stem from and float on the moving clouds, which formed a canopy over the valley below. Although I have been to various parts of the Himalayas, my visits never coincided with peak winter, which is why I have never experienced the snow there.

Having spent a memorable day, spanning less than twenty-four hours, inhaling the cheerfulness of the upland, I thanked Dalhousie for all that it had provided me with. After having hot and spicy samosas for breakfast, we departed from Dalhousie for Khajjiar in a bus that was not as packed as the one which had brought us here. Dalhousie and Chamba are about 45 kilometres apart, and Khajjiar lies midway.

Luckily, I got a window seat on the bus. It was a journey that took me through the beauty and wilderness of the hills on either side of the winding road that snaked through both gentle slopes and steep mountains. The hills were all covered in the viridian hue of the conifers, which were sometimes concealed by the translucent fog, and sometimes seen communing with the cool wind that filtered in through the hills. Khajjiar plateau was playing hide and seek because of the hairpin bends along the road. If ever a journey truly excited and awakened the traveller in me, it was this one! From one of the bus stops, an old man wearing a typical *Himachali* cap got on the bus, aided by his walking stick. The wrinkles on his cheeks fanned out from the corners of his toothless mouth. I also noticed an old woman sitting in a row ahead of him. Surprisingly, their faces and smile lines looked similar. Throughout this journey, I kept on collecting and treasuring unique pictures, from both inside and outside the bus.

Finally, we disembarked at Khajjiar, and I was awestruck at its first glance. Wow! Now that's a lovely plateau! The Khajjiar hill station has been described as a 'Mini Switzerland' by the Swiss envoy to India in the early 1990s on account of its similarity with Switzerland. Khajjiar is a small saucer-shaped plateau that contains a small lake, and it lies on the foothills of the Dhauladhar Ranges. The plateau at first glance was nothing less than a stunning dream destination; the deodar and pine forests that surrounded it, the lake in the middle, the blanket of green lawn that overspread the ground, the blue sky spanning a clear, large, green space below, and the feathery clouds that were moving in slow rhythmic motion in the sky. Although it was a sunny day, the glare and heat of the sun were not that intense.

Apart from the scenic views, Khajjiar had in store for visitors various activities one could engage in, such as a play area for children, trekking, adventurous sports like paragliding, and restaurants. Animals, including pets and commercial animals, were seen here and there. Rabbits and flower vases were available for rent as add-ons for instant photos. Horse riding was another sporty activity seen there. Paragliders were making their safe landings on the slopes of the green meadow. I recollected my paragliding experience in Manali, flying like a bird in the high sky above the green hills and valleys. Orbs carrying people at their core were rolling downhill through the meadows like soapy bubbles. It reminded me of the zorbing (also called globe-riding or orbing) that I had done while in Chhattisgarh about nine years ago. Balloons and cotton candies for sale added colour to the overall dreamscape. I lay down on the lawn that was dressed up in buffalo grass and gazed at the blue sky above.

Before I could truly delve into Khajjiar's soul, we had to catch the next bus to Chamba. I got up from the grassy ground, and smiling from deep within my heart, expressed my gratitude to the entire world for all the good fortunes and opportunities I have had. All of us walked towards the bus station. The Khajji Nag Temple is situated slightly apart. Built a millennium ago by the Chamba king Prithvi Singh, the temple derives its name from the serpent god (*Nag*) worshipped here. Horses continued carrying tourists along the main road. Our bus arrived, and we got on it, awaiting another set of unique impressions in Chamba.

The character of the landscape along the transit route gradually changed its colour and vigour; the tall pines and deodars, characteristic of the alpine landscape, disappeared from the immediate vicinity, and shrubs and short trees in hues of sap green and yellow ochre began to appear as picturesque frames across the slopes. The outside temperature slowly kept on rising, and I started to sweat. From a higher altitude, I had a bird's-eye view of the hill town of Chamba nestled in a river valley. With care, our bus descended the hills, from whose valley was heard the sound of a river, streaming towards the west. It was the Ravi, one of the five tributaries of the River Indus. I was all excited to experience Chamba firsthand, though I had already formed a preliminary impression from maps and images displayed in our seniors' studio at the School of Planning and Architecture (SPA).

Before becoming a part of Himachal Pradesh post-independence, Chamba had been governed by various rulers, including tribes, Rajputs, Pratiharas, and Sikhs, and it had also come under British control for nearly a hundred years. The ancient capital of the kingdom to the east of Chamba, named Brahampura (present day Bharmour), was founded by Maru in the 6th century in the valley of the Budhil River. Raja Sahilla Varman, who came to power in the 10th century, unified the territory of Chamba, which had been divided into fragments. He shifted the capital of the kingdom to a strategic location in the valley of the Ravi and named it Chamba after Champavati, his daughter.

Chamba is located at the confluence of the River Ravi and its tributary, the River Sal. It occupies the right bank of the Ravi, on a terraced topography. The natural advantages of being at an isolated location and the presence of high mountain ranges have granted it security throughout its history and saved it from severe invasions, though it has had conflicts with the neighbouring hill states. Chamba is connected to the rest of the world by roadways.

The density of the buildings on either side, which were initially scattered, gradually gave way to clusters as we approached Chamba. We crossed the bridge built across the Ravi, which was flowing in slow motion along the valley of the hill town. In no time, our bus reached the bus station located uphill, which was too small to accommodate the huge crowd there. After getting off the bus, we walked upwards along the avenue beside the *Chaugan*, a large open ground that sits in the heart of Chamba.

A glimpse of the entire town could be seen from the *Chaugan*; the Ravi and the mountains in its backdrop to the West, the part of the town seen downhill to the West of *Chaugan*, and another part seen uphill to its other sides. The eastern skyline of the town, as viewed from the northwestern corner of the *Chaugan*, was defined by the Akhand Chandi Palace and the mountains that seemed to soar from both sides of it.

On our way, we entered the Shri Hari Rai Temple, to the northwest of the *Chaugan*. It was a Nagara-style temple, built of stone and wood. Moving further, we came across a post office, where I bought some postcards. Dated 18.05.2016, I wrote on one: "*This is from Chamba, a small town in Himachal Pradesh. Still a lot left to explore. Let me see the rest of it. We just arrived here from Khajjiar, a plateau located on the way from Dalhousie to Chamba. Must go places...Entirely different landscape.*" The post box was much larger than any I had seen before. Posting the card, we continued ascending the road, which progressively became steeper as well as narrower.

We stopped on sighting the Akhand Chandi Palace, a sizeable structure that sits with its head high, to the North of the *Chaugan*. It was built in the late 18th century by Raja Umed Singh. With the additions done in successive years, it shows the influences from the architectural styles of the Mughals and the British. In the 1970s, the Himachal Pradesh Government bought the palace from the Royal family of Chamba and put it to a new use. It now accommodates the Government P.G. College and the District library. The Palace, beyond its forecourt, was out of bounds for visitors as it was a working day. We spent some time in that court, sitting on the benches beside a fountain. The arched doors and windows, the pilasters, and the rectangular windows adorn the otherwise plain exterior walls of the palace, which has a sloping roof as another striking feature. The later additions in the form of spaces and materials were obvious from the elevation of the palace. We continued walking along the streets that displayed structures belonging to various time periods.

Owing to its location in the Himalayas, the traditional architecture of Chamba was considerate of the local climatic factors and the seismic activity prevalent in the region. Thus, stone and wood, which were locally available, were used as the primary construction materials for both secular and religious structures, including houses and temples. The construction technique used was dry stone masonry, in which the building blocks of stones, in particular the interlocking ones, were put together without using mortar as a binder.

On our way, we entered the Lakshmi Narayan Temple complex, located to the northwest of the Akhand Chandi Palace. Raja Sahilla Varman built the main temple in this temple complex, and also the Champavati Temple, built in memory of his daughter, to the north of the *Chaugan*. Both temples were built in the Nagara-style of architecture. Like the Shri Hari Rai Temple, the temples in the Lakshmi Narayan Temple complex featured projecting entrances covered by sloping roofs. Another sloping roof was seen at a higher level than the one above the entrance. The sanctum of the temple was covered by an octagonal roof, with a small conical roof above, topped by a finial. The Sui Mata Temple, on the Shah Madar hill to the east of the town, was built in memory of Raja Sahilla Varman's wife, who, according to legend, had sacrificed her own life to bring water to Chamba. Thus, the Queen and the daughter of Raja Sahilla Varman have been deeply venerated by the *Chambyal* (the people of Chamba), and this royal trio occupies a prime position in the history and legends that are centred on Chamba.

The British rule in Chamba brought about various progressive reforms and developments. In the latter half of the 19th century, the urban architecture of Chamba was heavily transformed by the British. Those interventions in the built fabric comprised the construction of secular buildings (post office, hospital, library) and religious buildings (temples, churches), the construction of new roads and bridges (including the road to Dalhousie via Khajjiar), and the modification of the *Chaugan*s, among others. The *Chaugan*, meaning four-sided in Sanskrit, is the core of all the activities in the town, hosting events such as traditional fairs and festivals, cricket matches, and picnics. It has become an integral part of the social life of *Chambyal*. During the British period, five *Chaugan*s were merged to form an exceptionally huge *Chaugan* for recreational purposes. It was an enclosed and open-to-sky green space, shaded by avenue trees to the west, and by a mix of buildings and trees on the remaining sides. It was a lively place, wherein people were seen sitting alone, either simply enjoying the moment or reading, some were sitting in circles of friends and relatives, some were lying down on the ground, some were moving around, and the majority sought out the shade.

Unlike the previous destinations in the itinerary, Chamba had something special about it, other than its beauty, a great deal of which is contributed by its geographical location. Besides being a hill station, the first glance of the town offered some other images too, mainly that of a historic urban settlement. The cultural landscape of Chamba consists of different cultures, organically interlaced with and overlaid onto the natural landscape. Over the layers designed and defined by the natives from various parts of the sub-continent, the layer of British rule got imprinted on Chamba, and the town's current form is an eclectic architectural mix. For the residents of Chamba, the landscape has been an associative one. Under British rule, it also attained the form of a designed landscape. It serves as both a multi-layered historic hill settlement and a hill station modified to suit a foreign lifestyle. They present themselves as an inseparable whole, yet retaining the uniqueness of each.

Descending the sloping streets, shaded by buildings, we almost forgot about having food. It was only on reaching the *Chaugan* that we realized that it was past lunchtime. Lunch was over everywhere, even in a new restaurant that was inaugurated on the same day. The only exception was the restaurant run by the Himachal Pradesh Tourism Development Corporation, located beside the *Chaugan*, in its southeast corner. We had our lunch there and came out to the lawn lying adjacent to it in order to enjoy the sun. There was a children's play area at one end of the lawn, with a pair of swings and a see-saw. I sat on a swing, even though I knew it was meant for kids only. But I could not stop myself from sitting on it, as it reminded me of my splendid childhood. The food I ate might have been digested by the time I stopped swinging.

Coming out of the restaurant, we walked around the *Chaugan*, savouring cut watermelons. And from the shopping arcade near it, I shopped for a pair of Chamba's own handmade chappals and *Himachali* caps. I kept them in my backpack, and still it felt light! Chamba is also noted for its *Pahari* paintings; *Pahari* (or *Pahadi*) meaning hill people or mountain dwellers. It is a collective name for the style of paintings, mostly miniatures, which originated in the 17th century in Northwestern India, comprising a vast region including Chamba.

It was time to begin the journey back to Delhi. The long bus, which we got onto at the bus station, moved in a zig-zag pattern down along the curved roads that have been carefully carved out from the hillside. Since the luxurious bus had large glazed windows, the vivid scenes of the *pahad* (hill or mountain) could be seen clearly. While crossing the bridge this time, I noticed a fast-flowing Ravi, creating noisy splashes by hitting the boulders blocking its way. The gushing water was sparkling in the evening light that fell on the valley. The bus started to climb the hills on the other side of the valley. Even the bird's-eye view of Chamba began to fade from sight. In a terraced field atop the high, steep hill, a farmer and his oxen were struggling hard to plough the soil. The sun was slowly sinking into the river valley, between the dark green mountains of Himachal, to rise and shine well in Delhi.

16 BOMBAY-THANE, KAALI-PEELI, AND THE LOCAL TRAINS

"I recently watched the movie, *Slumdog Millionaire.* Are there slums everywhere in India? ", an overseas friend of mine asked me while we were in Germany. His question literally left me speechless. I told him, "There are, of course, pockets of slums here and there, like in most countries. But there is a lot more to see and feel once you are in India." It is quite unfortunate to find movies giving a completely negative image of what India is, intentionally or not. Mumbai, in particular, has been stereotyped as the hotspot of crime by movies that tell the stories of the so-called 'underworld' and those that portray the life of the underprivileged living in slums. Unfortunately, many viewers tend to generalize this to represent the whole of Mumbai. Added to this is the scarring memory of the 26/11 terror attacks. Anyway, much like the two sides of a coin, Mumbai has its own duality, with one side being brighter and more vibrant.

I went to Mumbai for the first time in 2011, with my classmates and professors, as part of a studio project during my undergraduate studies. There, we conducted case studies of apartments by eminent, mainstream architects to explore the design possibilities of high-rise buildings. The morning after our arrival, I realized our hotel was located quite close to the Taj Hotel (the Taj Mahal Palace) and the Gateway of India, which adorn the West Coast of India, right on the Arabian Sea. Keen to familiarize ourselves with the seafront, we set out even before sunrise.

In movies, I had often seen flocks of pigeons being fed by passersby, an image synonymous with the Gateway of India. Whenever I saw such images, I longed to feed the pigeons, watch them fly high up in the sky, and listen to the flap of their wings. As I had always wished, I was right there, with several hundred pigeons near the Gateway of India. I bought a packet of cereal and fed the pigeons. When I tried to touch one, that magical moment arrived; together they flew to the vast sky, making a noisy flutter. I felt happy to have ticked off one item on my wish list.

We moved ahead to the promenade along the sea to get a clear view of the sunrise. A few ships and boats were sailing on the sea, while others were docked. The major and minor establishments along the city's streets had already begun their day-to-day business. I sat on a low wall near the Gateway of India, relishing the panoramic view of the sea and of the seafront—the pigeons taking mesmerizing flights, people of different origins seeking life and work in the metropolis, the city's iconic black-and-yellow '*kaali-peeli*' taxis zipping through the streets, and the timeless heritage structures and soaring skyscrapers standing tall ashore.

That point on the seafront has a rich and eventful history, particularly during the British Raj. The Gateway of India was built in the early 20th century by reclaiming the land at Apollo Bunder. It commemorates the first visit of the British monarch, King George V, to India in 1911 for his coronation as Emperor of India. The Gateway served as a grand entry point to the country by sea for esteemed personnel during the British Raj.

And it was right from here that the last British troops left India in 1948, a year after Indian independence. Thus, this edifice holds a prominent place in the history of modern India, having served for about two and a half decades as a symbolic ceremonial entrance and exit gate for the colonial power.

Built in the Indo-Islamic style, fused with the regional architecture of Gujarat, the Gateway of India stands as a proud, iconic landmark in the city. It is a rectangular structure with arched openings. The longer side to the southeast forms the main entry from the sea. Four turrets rise above both sides of the main central arched passageway. The façade features detailing such as the ornamental design of the *jali* screens (stone lattice work) set around the arched openings, and the brackets supporting the projecting cornices. The entire composition looks more striking at night when it is illuminated by the city lights. Tourists, locals, vendors, photographers, boatmen, among many others, throng its premises. Jetties near it provide operational ferry services to various spots in Mumbai.

The Taj Mahal Palace Hotel, another product of the thoughtful fusion of Indian and other architectural styles (including Gothic, Neo-Classical, and Islamic), stands next to the Gateway of India, facing the sea from across the promenade. Built in 1903, it is a luxury hotel that is part of the priceless heritage buildings of Indo-Saracenic architectural style dotting the seafront. Even 120 years after its opening, the Taj continues to host and entertain guests. The addition of a twenty-storey high-rise structure after about seventy years of its construction stands distinct from the original fabric, which is six-storeyed. The Taj, despite the damage it sustained a few years back, regained its illustrious status and radiance.

On all the days I had spent in Mumbai, I would step out with my friends, early in the morning and late in the evening, either to the same spots or new ones. And while travelling on the bus to the case study locations, I got glimpses of the various identities, symbols and images associated with and attributed to the city of Mumbai. On every such trip, back and forth, we travelled along the road in front of the Chhatrapati Shivaji Maharaj Terminus (CSMT), which was inscribed as a UNESCO World Heritage Site in 2004 in the cultural category. As a masterpiece of Indo-Saracenic architecture, the CSMT demonstrates both the architectural features of the Victorian Gothic Revival in India and the characteristics of traditional Indian architecture. The CSMT, opened in 1888, was built over 10 years, with British architects collaborating with Indian craftsmen. They produced a finely blended structure featuring architectural elements such as spires, pointed arches, towers, and turrets.

I was so excited to see the Bombay Stock Exchange (BSE) on Dalal Street, which I had seen only in business news. With limited time at our disposal, we did not go far for shopping. The Colaba Causeway was one of the commercial spots easily accessible from our hotel. From there, I bought a string of wooden beads with vibrant colours. Colaba was formed by merging two islands, which were originally inhabited by *Koli*s, the indigenous community engaged in fishing and agriculture. In later years, it came under the Portuguese and the British. Rising land prices in Colaba resulted from the establishment of the commercial centre in the early 19th century, large-scale development, and considerable land reclamation. The native *Koli*s experienced resultant alienation and are now pushed to the edges.

We spent the entire forenoon on a very pleasant day in the designed open spaces on Malabar Hill, one of Mumbai's highest points and green spaces. That place was a forest back in the 18th century. Because of some adverse incidents that had occurred in the 19th century, including epidemics and the Great Fire of 1803 in the fort area of Mumbai, the city's elites, including natives and the British, moved uphill and settled on Malabar Hill. Besides the natural security it offers, Malabar Hill is a vantage point which gives a bird's-eye view of the port city and of the sea.

In 1880, as part of linking lakes for water supply in Mumbai, an artificial reservoir was built on Malabar Hill. The Hanging Gardens, also known as the Sir Pherozeshah Mehta Gardens, sit on this reservoir. The Kamala Nehru Park, named after the wife of Pandit Jawaharlal Nehru, was built as part of the Hanging Gardens in the mid-20th century. It houses a shoe-shaped 'Boot House', inspired by the nursery rhyme, '*There was an old woman who lived in a shoe*', which has been a prime attraction for kids coming to the park. From the garden, I had a brief look at the beach downhill. It was a spectacular view of Marine Drive, with the busy Mumbai city to its left and the seemingly calm Arabian Sea to its right. The lights along the promenade have earned Marine Drive the nickname 'Queen's Necklace'. Hundreds of little black stones and rock pieces scattered on the shore were being bathed in the white foam produced by the slow-paced waves arising from the Back Bay, an inlet of the Arabian Sea. The evening rays of the sun made those stones shimmer like diamonds. The tangible and intangible products of different time periods embodied in the city's tapestry, the sand subject to countless cycles of deposition and erosion on the shore, and the water and waves of the sea—all sang the saga of Mumbai in unison.

I enjoyed travelling via the Bandra-Worli Sea Link (officially called the Rajiv Gandhi Sea Link) just as much as the walk along the promenade edging the sea. The Sea Link is a cable-stayed bridge connecting Bandra in Western Mumbai with Worli in Southern Mumbai, designed to reduce the travel time between the two considerably.

The same day, I saw the forested area on Malabar Hill where the Tower of Silence of the Zoroastrians (or the Parsee community) was located. The concept behind this funerary tower, called *Dakhma* (in Persian), was new to me, and it sounded a little strange initially. Inside the circular tower, the corpses of the dead are exposed to scavenger birds like vultures, which consume them. Its scientific reasoning is that the final disposition should not cause any harm to the elements of nature, like wind (or air), fire, earth, or water, considered sacred by the Zoroastrians. Though the approaches of most religions differ, they in essence teach the need for being one with nature.

This expedition to Mumbai ended in less than a week, leaving me with the feeling that I had seen Mumbai only in bits and pieces and was yet to explore the city.

I returned to Mumbai after four and a half years, precisely two weeks after the completion of my post-graduation. I booked a morning flight to Mumbai to see my dear friend and classmate at SPA Delhi, Sneha. We were so thrilled to see each other at the Mumbai airport. She gave me a friendly hug, saying, "Welcome to Mumbai!" Exchanging brief words, we proceeded to the airport metro.

When the metro passed through an elevated track, I sighted a slum that was climbing onto the ridges of hills, after having saturated the plains. These are the instances that make us think about a myriad of aspects of life. When equality and equity remain distant from some sections of the population, they become underprivileged and marginalized. This leads to disparities in opportunities and representation. The alienated, having no means to make ends meet, will often use public properties with common rights that lack individual ownership. Say, for example, those who cannot afford to have land properties due to the rising real estate prices will probably occupy the common lands, which in legal terms is deemed 'illegal encroachment'. It is a sad reality that, even after seventy-eight years of independence, the schemes for development and financial aid designed for the poor in Indian society have not fully reached the 'real' beneficiaries. Consequently, some people remain in poverty for their entire lives, and in some cases, for generations. A nation truly prospers only when it empowers every citizen in all senses. We are in dire need of visionaries, leaders, and change-makers who can take sensible steps in the right direction to uplift the poor as well.

It was time to change our mode of transport to Mumbai's own local train, officially known as the suburban trains, in order to reach Thane, located around 25 kilometres to the northeast of Mumbai. At the railway station, there were people rushing to their offices, students to schools and colleges, and cobblers busy polishing the shoes of those who wanted that extra shine and neat look. While entering the train to Thane, I recollected a two-year-old scene at the Rajiv Chowk metro station in New Delhi, awaiting the train to Mehrauli. Being frustrated with moving around in the crowd, I murmured, "I want to get rid of this crowd!" My friend Ruchita laughed and replied, "In Mumbai, you simply have to wait in front of the train's door. The crawling crowd will take you inside." Hearing this, Sneha nodded as if it were true. And of course it is! They were right! I swear! The crowd swept us into the ladies' compartment—me, my luggage, and my friend. Luckily, in the middle of the journey, I got a seat somewhere and looked around for Sneha, who had been missing for a short while.

Suburban trains are for commuters travelling from the suburbs to the central city. There are certain safety concerns about these trains. They stop for only 10 seconds and run at intervals of about 5 minutes. The open doors pose a genuine threat to new users. Sometimes overcrowding, especially during peak hours, have resulted in casualties. Despite all that, most of Mumbai is dependent on them.

Inside the compartment, there were women from all walks of life, carrying the tools of their trades: school and college students with backpacks; working women with handbags; fruit and vegetable vendors with baskets; and matriarchs and homemakers with groceries or stationery. Having noticed that I had been observing the people around, Sneha told me, "I used to catch local trains every day to my college, with sheets, a roll-pack, and a model". "Seriously!?" I asked her, as her words did not convince me. She just smiled. I wiped off my sweat with a handkerchief. As a daily commuter by bus, I know the struggles. But it was nothing compared to Sneha's experience in local trains back in college.

I was so happy to have travelled from Mumbai to Thane by train, as it is connected to a milestone event in the history of Indian Railways. My father used to share with us several historical facts known to him, and he had told me that Bombay-Thana was the route of the first passenger train in India, opened up by the British in 1853. The British spelt it Thana, and 'Thane' replaced it in 1996. The terminal in Bombay (now Mumbai) was called Bori Bunder. Three decades after its opening, it was rebuilt as Victoria Terminus. Later, it was renamed the Chhatrapati Shivaji Maharaj Terminus (CSMT) after Chhatrapati Shivaji Maharaj, the great Maratha ruler of the 17th century. For nearly two centuries since its inception, millions have been using this service, which has become an indispensable part of their daily lives. Historical significance adds another dimension to the sense of a place, reminding people of the long miles covered by those of a bygone era.

Finally, we reached the historically significant Thane railway station. We walked along a footbridge and a few streets before reaching her apartment. All the roads were drenched by the rain that fell the day before. Reaching her home, I greeted her mother, kept my luggage in a corner of the hall, and took a quick home tour, before having our breakfast together. Her family and I knew each other in advance, as they used to visit her while we were doing our Master's in Delhi. Through the window of her bedroom, I saw the Thane station and the footbridge at a distance. Soon, that window became my outlook tower, offering a clear and wide view of the townscape of Thane. Exhausted after losing a night's sleep to the flight journey, I took a short nap in the morning itself, which was quite unusual in my daily routine.

After lunch, we went to the local market near Thane. It was reminiscent of Sadar Bazaar, a wholesale market in Old Delhi. I went there with Ruchita and Sneha to shop for essentials for the fresher's party organized for our juniors. The moment we landed at Sadar Bazaar, out of extreme excitement, both of them freaked out. With their eyes wide-open and sparkling, they cried out in chorus, "This one looks exactly like the markets back home!" And their finding was absolutely right!

After making quick purchases, we took the local train that goes to Dadar. Mumbai's markets are worth exploring and experiencing. I enjoyed the walk along the commercial neighbourhood in Dadar, stopping at shops selling a diverse range of products, and shopping for the ones that I had wanted.

Tired of walking, we both sat on a low wall edging the Chhatrapati Shivaji Maharaj Park and the paved pedestrian walkway. The park, which serves as an open ground or *maidan*, has hosted various events, including socio-political gatherings and sports, since its opening in 1925. It had been the venue for the meetings of freedom fighters during the pre-independence period and had also seen the protests calling for a separate Marathi-speaking state of Maharashtra. The park has been a prime location for events organized by Shiv Sena, a political party that originated in Maharashtra. It has also been the playground of several legendary Indian cricketers, including Sachin Tendulkar. Being popular destinations in the city for all age groups, both the park and its surrounding area create a vibrant atmosphere. The trees lining the pedestrian walkway provided shade to those occupying the seats and the park benches along the perimeter of the park. A hawker was selling umbrellas of different shades, textures, and sizes near the pedestrian path, most of which were suspended from above for better visibility, adding to the aesthetics of the entire urban setting.

Gaining some energy, we rose from the low wall and moved towards the seafront. The part of the shore where we reached was deserted. A sign cautioned us it was a no-entry area, a preventive measure adopted by the concerned authorities. It was full of tetrapods, the concrete blocks used to dissipate waves and to arrest the erosion of the shoreline by high tides. Exiting the lonely shore, we walked back to the bustling streets of Dadar. Walking continued until we stepped into the Church of Our Lady of Salvation (also called the Portuguese Church or the Salvacao Church). It was originally built by the Portuguese in the 16th century. The structure seen now was designed by architect Charles Correa in the 1970s, breaking conventional ideas of church design. And this is the place where he rests in peace. The church also features paintings by Indian artists M.F. Husain and Anjolie Ela Menon.

A *kaali-peeli* took us to the nearest train station. These black and yellow coloured 'Premier Padmini' taxis that had been restlessly plying on the thoroughfares of Mumbai, disappeared from the streets roughly three years ago. Its top was painted yellow (*peela* in Hindi) to aid in its identification from a distance. The lower portion was painted black (*kaala* in Hindi), as taxis, being public carriers, were more prone to getting dirty and stained. The move to withdraw them from the roads came after the phasing out of the red-coloured diesel-powered double-decker buses from the public transport of Mumbai. Their discontinuation followed a 2013 city regulation mandating the decommissioning of taxis once they reached 20 years of age. The last of the Premier Padmini cars registered as a kaali-peeli was in 2003, thus meeting the 20-year age limit for taxis in the year 2023.

Besides the highly acclaimed structures in the cityscape, including the CSMT, Gateway of India, and Taj Hotel, Mumbai's identity can undeniably be said to be incomplete without the presence of *kaali-peeli*s. For they have also, over the years, become the icons and symbols of the city. Leaving behind sentimental value and emotional attachments shared by the people and the city, *kaali-peeli*s took their final ride in 2023. They had been serving the city of Mumbai for six illustrious decades since the start of their production in India in the latter half of the 20th century.

The transport sector of Mumbai may undergo a complete overhaul, driven by the introduction of new technologies. Even so, the memories of the major modes of public transport that had once ruled the roads of the city, like the double-decker buses and the *kaali-peeli*s, would remain forever in the hearts of the people.

Travelling on local trains was still the toughest part of my navigation in Mumbai. If anyone wanted to exit the train at a particular station, she (as we used to travel in the ladies' compartment) would come near the door two stations ahead. Signalling her intention to disembark, she would begin pushing towards the door. I got annoyed when a young lady shoved me while I was standing on the edge of the doorway, with three or four people ahead of me. People like me, who want to keep away from crowds, will be put in real trouble on Mumbai's local trains, unless they are adept at or willing to adapt to them.

When it drizzled in the evening, Sneha took me for a stroll to Thane Creek, an inlet of the Arabian Sea. Marshy land and mangroves edged the river, beside which was located a park, where boys played cricket, and groups of young people and older adults gathered to unwind. Thane is blessed with several lakes (*Talao*) for which it is also known as the 'City of Lakes'. The intermittent rain during the monsoon left the streets soaked all the time. While returning to her home, I bought a small can of juice made of *kokum* (Garcinia indica). It is a dark purple fruit from a tropical evergreen tree native to the Konkan region in the Western Ghats, which also stretches to the state of Maharashtra.

The next day, we planned to go to the Elephanta Caves. Though travelling in a local train was a significant challenge, especially during the morning rush, I felt happy having reached the historic CSMT in one of them. While many historic buildings are now adaptively reused, CSMT has continued to serve the ever-increasing needs of passengers for over 140 years while retaining most of its original fabric; a testament to the structural integrity and engineering excellence of this late-19th century marvel. Leaving the terminus, we walked all the way to the jetty at Apollo Bunder. The streets were nearly empty, as it was a few hours before the shops and offices opened. The sheer scale and splendour of the fort area's rich heritage filled me with wonder. At one point, I felt we were on a heritage walk.

We halted at the Horniman Circle, which was enclosed by a ring of buildings. At its centre is located the Horniman Circle Garden, a large open space of 2.5 acres, built in the late 19th century and named after Benjamin Horniman, the editor of the Bombay Chronicle newspaper. To the east of the Circle is located the Town Hall, which houses, notably, the Asiatic Society of Mumbai, an institution founded by the British lawyer and jurist, Sir James Mackintosh, in the early 19th century. The aim of the Asiatic Society was to acquire and promote useful knowledge about the people, culture, language, literature, and other aspects of India and of the Orient. It is a colonnaded building, with a series of steps leading towards the main entrance, and the elevation was reminiscent of Classical architecture, featuring a triangular pediment, columns to the front, and a portico, among others.

Our refreshing morning walk ended at the jetty, near the Gateway of India. While waiting for the ferry service that would commence at 9 AM, we had an instant photo taken by a photographer there, who captured us with the Gateway of India in the background. Booking two tickets for the ferry ride, we got onto the deck of the boat. And we set out on the voyage to Elephanta Island, about 10 kilometres or an hour's travel to the east of Mumbai city. Both small boats and giant ships were floating on the Arabian Sea; her waters looked grey, reflecting the rain clouds looming above. On our way, we passed by Jawahar Dweep, which houses a marine oil terminal. From far across the sea, I got a sneak peek of the green-clad Elephanta Island. Oriented along the southwest-northeast axis, it comprises two hillocks with an altitude of about 150 metres; namely Cannon Hill to the southwest and Stupa Hill to the northeast, separated by a narrow valley in between.

Elephanta is an inhabited island, with about 1200 islanders distributed across three villages, namely Shetbunder, Morabunder, and Rajbunder (or Gharapuri), at the northwest, northeast, and southern ends of the island, respectively. The island was earlier known as Gharapuri (meaning the place of caves), with the original settlers being called *Gharapuri*s. The Portuguese renamed it Elephanta after the stone sculpture of an elephant found at the entrance of the Rajbunder Jetty (located to the south of the island), where they had disembarked. In the late 19th century, following an unsuccessful British attempt to transport it to England, the elephant sculpture fell and broke. After reassembling the broken pieces, the sculpture has been on display at the entrance of the Victoria Gardens Museum in Mumbai, now known as the Veermata Jijabai Bhonsale Udyan (named after the mother of Chhatrapati Shivaji Maharaj).

The island is archaeologically significant as well. It comprises ancient remains dating back to the 2nd Century BCE, as is clear from the two unexplored and unexcavated stupas still buried in Stupa Hill. The two cannons in Cannon Hill stand as relics of the

Portuguese occupation.

I expected the island to be a secluded one with very minimal footfall. On approaching the Shetbunder Jetty, I could see a long stretch of commercial activities, contrary to my anticipation. Residents of the island who had taken up vending as a livelihood, stationed at the jetty, were eagerly awaiting the first incoming boat of the day. They earned a living through the sale of pickles, sweets, fruits, hats, and the like to the ferried tourists. We alighted from the boat that was docked at the jetty. From there, a toy train took us to the base of the island. Those willing to walk could walk the 600-metre pathway alongside the toy train's narrow-gauge track.

From the base, we had to walk uphill, climbing a long flight of about 120 steps, to reach the caves. If unable to walk, people carrying palanquins would come to our rescue. Stalls selling trinkets and curios such as jewellery, artefacts, souvenirs, and toys lined the stepped pathway, where the business was on a larger scale than the one at the jetty. Monkeys would sometimes steal or snatch these items, which would then be retrieved by the hawkers through a clever chase. Fearing the aggressive antics of the monkeys, we quickly collected the entry tickets from the main entrance and headed towards the location of the caves.

From the main entrance, three pathways emerge. One to the right goes upwards to the two cannons on Cannon Hill. The central one leads to the Main Caves numbered 1-5, on Cannon Hill, and near the main entrance. The other, to the left, goes downwards to the Elephanta Dam and Lake Garden, and further to the Caves numbered 6 and 7, and the two stupas on Stupa Hill. There are altogether seven rock-cut caves in Elephanta that were sculpted between the mid-5th and 6th centuries. The Main Caves 1-5 are associated with Hinduism, mostly of Shaivite beliefs, and the remaining two with Buddhism.

The Great Cave 1 (or simply Cave 1), among the Main Caves

1-5 on Cannon Hill, is the most prominent of the Elephanta Caves. It is the largest too, measuring 39 metres from the front entrance to the rear end. It has porticos on the three open sides, facing North, East, and West, the main entrance being from the North side. Huge panels with high reliefs representing the different forms and expressions of Lord *Shiva*, namely *Nataraja* (Lord of dance) and *Yogishvara* (Lord of *Yoga*), flank both sides of this northern entrance. The *mandapa* (hall), which is supported by pillars, has a *garbhagriha* (sanctum sanctorum) at the western end, allowing the *Shiva linga* shrine to face the rising sun.

The cave also encloses an open temple, aligned in the north-south direction, on the southern wall facing the main northern entrance. At its centre is found the '*Trimurti Sadashiva*' (three-faced *Shiva*), a 7 metre-tall sculpture, which is an outstanding work of rock art in India. The central face and the two profile faces of the sculpture depict three aspects of Shiva: the Creator, the Preserver, and the Destroyer. Both sides of the *Trimurti Sadashiva* sculpture are decorated by friezes (sculpted panels) with the theme of *Ardhanarishvara* to the East and that of the *Gangadhara* to the West. The shrine at the eastern entrance of the cave is related to Shaktism, even though the cave depicts themes mostly from the life of Lord *Shiva*. In fact, the cult of *Shiva* pervades the entire island, as the structural temples within villages and other areas are all dedicated to *Shiva*.

Among the Caves 2-5, some were unfinished, some had missing parts, the structures and artworks in some were badly damaged, and some had been reconstructed and restored. The layout and planning of the caves in Elephanta represent an important development in rock-cut architecture: integrating Hindu spiritual beliefs and symbology; featuring distinct spaces, pillars, and the provision of a sanctum sanctorum with a *sarvatobhadra* plan (sanctum with four functional doors in cardinal directions). Adapted from the legendary narrative related to

Hinduism, the sublime rock-cut art—consisting of sculptures, friezes, and reliefs—illustrates the various themes through a fine assemblage of form, expression, symbolism, representation, and detailing.

About 200 metres away from the Main Caves, and at the edge of Stupa Hill, are located Caves 6 and 7, which are associated with Buddhism. Cave 6 has a portico with four pillars and three chambers at its rear. The central chamber is a shrine, and the other two are cells for monks. Excavation of Cave 7 was halted due to structural issues.

The sheer dimension of the colossal rock-cut caves and the stone sculptures is so huge that we find ourselves extremely insignificant in front of them. I was truly astonished by the way they were carved from a rough medium. A lot of questions flashed through my mind. "How did people come here? How could they chisel and streamline such tremendous forms and shapes using only the manual tools and primitive machinery available in those times?" The peaceful yet powerful minds gained through their dedication and meditation might have made them capable of producing priceless and noteworthy works with their bare hands. Creativity and craftsmanship levels are not always tied to the abundance of modern facilities provided for the production of artwork.

The sun was about to reach overhead when we finished seeing all the caves. We climbed down the 120-odd steps, either side of which were lined with *Gharapuri* vendors. Since 1987, when the Elephanta Caves were inscribed on the UNESCO World Heritage List, the villagers have been benefiting from the protected status of the island, which has become a prime spot for heritage and tourism. The livelihoods of *Gharapuri*s include tourism, fishing, and boat repairing. Nowadays, most of them earn a living through tourism, running small-scale businesses along the access route, right from the base of the island, leading up to the caves.

Several factors limit the lives and livelihoods of the villagers: the seasonal nature of tourism; the limited number and strict timings of the ferry rides; the closure of ferry rides and the government-set limitations on other marine activities for three months during the Southwest monsoon; the prohibition of certain activities within the prohibited and regulated zones falling in the buffer zone of the protected island; and the absence of basic infrastructure including hospitals. Private fishing boats (or vessels) come to their rescue when the ferry is closed for the day or shut down during the Southwest monsoon.

We had our lunch on the island itself and ferried back to Mumbai at 12:30 PM, which was the first ferry ride of the day to the mainland. To avoid the harsh sun for an hour on the deck of the boat, we took shelter in the cabin. Though we evaded the sun, we could not save ourselves from the waters of the sea. As if to make us laugh, the sea was playing pranks with the boat by splashing water onto everyone. We both got drenched, even though we were occupying the seats near the central aisle. Mainland Mumbai gave a warm welcome to the visitors arriving by sea at the Gateway of India. At the jetty, people were running madly to get into the *kaali-peeli*s, which could hardly get a rest amidst the busy schedule of India's financial capital.

We headed back to Thane. And I blamed myself for having put myself once again in a local train. Resting at home for a little while, we went out to shop at the nearby market. I bought a new dress and had it altered at a small tailor shop I spotted by the side of the street. The shop had a sewing machine and a tailor working on it. He was wearing his measuring tape around his neck, and he seemed to be an extended and integral part of the sewing machine. Together with his machine, he occupied an extremely small space, which was barely two square metres. The ill effects of space constraints were reflected in his overall attitude and mannerisms, which might also have been affected by other issues only known to him.

The next day was a special occasion in Maharashtra, celebrated as '*Vat Purnima*' (meaning full moon related to the Banyan Tree). It was on this day that the legendary character Savitri had saved her husband Satyavaan from *Yamaraj* (God of death). In memory of this event, married Hindu women fast from dawn to dusk to pray for their husbands' longevity and well-being. They would go to temples to offer prayers and tie bands of sacred threads around the *Vat Vriksha* (Banyan Tree). The aim is to bring auspiciousness into their lives by seeking the blessings of the *Trimurti* or Trinity God (*Brahma*, *Vishnu*, and *Shiva*), who they believe inhabit the tree. Families would prepare special food and bring gifts for their neighbours and friends. That day, Sneha's mother was also wearing a traditional sari in the Marathi style, and after her visit to the temple, she served us the special food and sweets that she had prepared.

That being an auspicious day, I did not want to start it with a frustrating local train journey. Thus, for the day's outing, we opted for an air-conditioned bus of the State Government. The reward was a 'cool' and joyful journey on reserved seats in an uncongested bus, sparing us from the heat and humidity outside. After one and a half hours, we landed at the Sanjay Gandhi National Park (also called the Borivali National Park) in Borivali, which is about 27 kilometres west of Thane. It was established in the latter half of the 20th century, and it was renamed after Sanjay Gandhi towards its close. This protected forest, in a hilly terrain within the city limits of Mumbai, boasts the natural wealth of flora and fauna, as well as the cultural wealth of rock-cut caves dating back around two millennia.

Getting off the bus, we entered the park, eating bananas and enjoying salted berries and mangoes bought near the entrance. We collected the tickets for the safari and the Kanheri Caves. The

'Tiger and Lion Safari' was being conducted in the recreational and educational zone inside the Park, called Krishnagiri Upavan. It was with great excitement that I got onto the bus, which was secured with grills all around its glazed windows. Even though it was my maiden safari, it turned out to be a dismal one, as the lions, tigers and their partners were kept in enormous cages. It was at odds with the safaris I had seen in videos on wildlife, where animals would come near to people sitting in open vehicles. Seeing us 'peeping' through the barred glazed window, the lions and tigers would have felt sad, as we also were travelling in a 'cage', with the only difference being that we were moving on wheels. After half an hour or so, we reached the Kanheri Caves' entry point at the base of the hills.

Kanheri is derived from *Krishnagiri* (in Sanskrit, meaning 'black mountain'). The 109 Buddhist caves here were hewn out of the basaltic cliff by monks between the 1st century BCE and the 10th century CE. The Kanheri Caves had served as a Buddhist monastery, learning centre, and pilgrimage site. Most of these caves on the hillside were the Buddhist monks' *Vihara*s, meaning cells or small chambers for living, studying, and meditation. They were compact ones with single cells, having an entrance portico with pillars of square or octagonal shafts. Other larger ones were *Chaitya*s, a worship hall with a stupa at one end. The caves also display remarkable artworks by the monks as sculptures, reliefs, inscriptions, and paintings.

Climbing up the hills, along the steps that started all the way from the base, was tedious and energy-intensive. I was feeling bored and hopeless, especially after the safari, until I saw the first cave in the series, Cave 1. It was a *Vihara* built on two levels, with two pillars at the entrance portico. Caves 2 through 4 follow Cave 1 in a continuous line, located further north.

Cave 3, the Great Chaitya cave, is the most important of the caves here. A flight of steps leads to an enclosed forecourt.

Reliefs and sculptures embellish the enclosure on either side of the entrance. There is an inscription at the entrance to the forecourt. Two statues of Buddha in the standing posture, measuring 7 metres in height, adorn both sides of the entrance to the cave. At the entrance portico, two pillars stand tall, with five openings above them. There are two chambers to the left of the portico, one entered from inside the other. The wall facing the forecourt displays elaborate carvings. A large arched window rests above the entrance doorway to the hall from the portico. The hall has a plain stupa at the apsidal end, with 34 pillars around the nave and the stupa, and has a barrel-vaulted roof above. The capitals of most pillars are ornately sculpted.

Cave 4 is to the left of the Great Chaitya cave. It has a stupa enclosed by a small circular chamber, accessed through steps. Cave 2 is to the right of the Great Chaitya cave. It is open to the front and has 3 stupas inside small chambers, which are arranged from north to south. My eyes were delighted, encountering cave after cave, differing in scale and form. The caves and sculptures at Elephanta are monumental and more embellished. The ones in Kanheri seemed to be built to an intimate, human scale, and minimally adorned, whereas the caves of an earlier period in Kanheri are rather plain.

Kanheri Caves also demonstrate the water management systems that sustained the Buddhist monastery there. Various techniques were employed to conserve water in the cliff, such as rock-cut water cisterns along the sides of the forecourts of the caves, punctures on the court's floor, and rock-cut channels above the caves.

Monkeys were a real nuisance here as well, as in most other tourist spots elsewhere! Carefully, I climbed the hill, minding the monkeys and the steep drops beside the steps cut along the cliff. Reaching the summit, I was spellbound by the panoramic, 360-degree views featuring hills clad in green and ochre around. On the distant horizon, several hills were visible, fringed by an array of high-rise buildings—the offspring of urban sprawl from nearby areas. Those buildings of assorted sizes and shapes seemed like an army camping at the territorial boundary, ready to attack and conquer the tranquillity and serenity of the wildlife at any time. Human-wildlife conflicts have been a major issue raised from various parts of India, where the boundaries of human settlements and those of the wild intersect and interact. And most of the time, it happens either when humans gradually extend their occupation and encroach upon the range of the wild, or when resources go scarce in the wild.

Nature was gearing up for another downpour, judging by the signs around. On the hilltop, the puddles on the rocky surface reflected the disturbed sky. To reach their shelters before the rains, hundreds of birds flocked together, creating a stunning sight. Heavy winds continued trying to blow me down, but I endured their dramatic act. Within a few seconds, lightning occurred, tearing apart the clouds that had turned grey by then. The hilltop, being the highest point on the cliff, would become vulnerable and unsafe if it were struck by subsequent lightning events. Before the 'light and sound show' became violent, we retraced the rock-cut steps to the base of the hill.

On the way back to Thane, we entered a mall and spent about an hour there. After reaching home, Sneha took me for a walk in the neighbourhood, while it was still raining at night. I tried a few varieties of *pani-puri*, from a shop run by a couple who lived nearby. They prepared and served the different combinations of *pani-puri* as quickly as possible, each taking barely around thirty seconds. Their son, who came back after his tuition, joined them in their family business and helped them with the cleaning phase. I wondered whether they could even breathe during the peak hours of demand and supply!

Thane was in the shower for the whole of the next day. After watching a movie at a nearby theatre, we spared some time for shopping in the local market. I found a *mehandiwala* (one who makes designs with *mehandi* or *henna*) on the pedestrian path, sitting opposite the market building. He had a boxful of *mehandi*, a small stool to sit on, and a catalogue demonstrating various designs and templates. As part of our makeover for our classmate's wedding in Coimbatore, we decided to get *mehandi* done on our palms. As soon as he started his design, it started raining heavily. All of us in the market, including the two of us, and the *mehandiwala* with his tools and equipment, ran inside the market building. We found a place in one corner, where he set up his portable shop again and continued plotting his creative designs onto our palms.

It was still raining when we came out of the market building. To get home before it got too late, we had no choice but to open our umbrellas and walk in the rain. With one hand raised and stretched out of the umbrella's coverage, and the other holding our purchases and the umbrella itself, we walked along the streets of Thane. The falling droplets created ripples on the soaked ground, and we splashed our feet in the water that had filled the road's potholes.

17 THE CITIES OF AURO

After celebrating our friend's wedding in Karur, near Coimbatore, eight of us travelled to Pondicherry on a public transport bus, a journey spanning nearly five hours. In those days, while travelling, I was obsessed with getting the front seat in vehicles, as they naturally offered clear, uninterrupted views of the routes being covered. That day, I had to wait for two hours to get there. When I was about to sit on it, the driver told me to occupy the one just behind it, as the very front seat was reserved for the conductor. The bus, on its way, was taking on more passengers and goods. When most of the passengers got off with their belongings, the driver informed me that my dearest seat had become vacant. I occupied it at that instant itself.

The bus, on exiting the urban limits, gradually sped up. I glanced at the driver, who became reckless upon entering low-traffic areas. He was wearing sunglasses and had a handkerchief tied around his neck. With the 100 dB horn (I suspect it was even louder than that!), he was scaring the cyclists and the motor-cyclists who seemed anxious to share the road with our bus. To escape from his 'unique way' of rash driving, they brilliantly changed tracks, and were sometimes riding off the road, on the unpaved, non-demarcated pedestrian pathways. Seeing all this, I grabbed the handgrip and clung to it tightly with both hands. As if my prayers had been heard and answered, rain poured down, and the odometer reading gradually dipped. The driver put the wipers on, which interrupted the view a bit. To feel the rain, I left the window shutter open. Seeing me enjoying the trip, one of my friends occupying a nearby seat asked, "Why are you so obsessed with the front seat?" Instead of explaining myself, I asked her to experience it once. We exchanged our seats, after which she did not even ask me for a swap. The bus-ride ended at Pondicherry in the evening, and we proceeded to our place of stay in Auroville, which is located ten kilometres further north.

It was getting really dark when we neared the Auroville Youth Camp. In the absence of streetlights, that too along the winding lanes, the place appeared to be a thick forest. At one of the turns along the way, our auto-rickshaw's headlights illuminated a girl standing by a wall, filling us with a chill. A second look at the girl helped allay all our fears. Oh, my God! It was just graffiti! After one or two turns, we reached the Youth Camp. Once done with the registration process, we had our dinner and proceeded to our rooms; one on the first floor, right above the office, and another in the building next to it.

I stayed in the first-floor room, an L-shaped bedroom with an attached bathroom and an open terrace. It was a thatched building with exposed brickwork, punctured by openings that were devoid of any window panels. Despite my efforts to find a blank wall for my bed, the room's many openings made it impossible. Left with no choice and losing all hope, I settled into a bed adjacent to one of the windows, all of which had nothing but a curtain. Before going to sleep, I made sure to tie the lower end of the curtain to the sill with some small, solid objects. After making the necessary arrangements for my safety, I lay down straight, closed my eyes, pulled the blanket, and took a vow that I would be vigilant till dawn to keep the blanket in its place. The fatigue that had mounted up after a long journey during the day and the soothing winds that trespassed through the curtains at night were enough to make me fall asleep quickly. Anyhow, I kept my promise until I woke up the next morning.

What seemed to be a thick forest through the window last night turned into a thoughtfully designed landscaped garden when seen in the morning. The smiles of the flowers on creepers, and lotuses and lilies in small tanks, made the morning fabulous. Inside a thatched pavilion in the garden, I saw a girl doodling in her sketchbook. She was an architect turned designer, and a friend of my friend Ruchita, who had come to join us for the trip. With only two days available for everyone to spend in Pondicherry, we changed our itinerary. We postponed the exploration of Auroville until the next day and brought forward that of Pondicherry. Soon, everyone got ready for the drive towards Pondicherry. At one turning, I noticed the image of the girl on the wall, which had scared me off last night. Some works of art can really be disquieting when seen in unexpected places at odd times. After passing several more such surprises and chance discoveries, we reached the city of Pondicherry.

Pondicherry is the capital city of the Union Territory (UT) of Puducherry. The UT comprises four districts that are geographically scattered across the South of India: Mahe on the Western coast of India abutting the Arabian Sea, Pondicherry and Karaikal on the Eastern Coast of India abutting the Bay of Bengal, and Yanam in the delta of the Godavari River that eventually joins the Bay of Bengal. Being surrounded by the state of Tamil Nadu on all sides but the East, which is bounded by the Bay of Bengal, Pondicherry draws a lot from the Tamil culture, apart from the obvious French influences. Despite being an integral part of the Indian Union since 1954 (the year of de facto transfer of the French possessions in India), Pondicherry still continues to uphold its French administrative and cultural legacy.

The bright red *kepi* (headgear) still worn by the police force in the city is a minor example.

Pondicherry was quite familiar to me through my Urban Design studio during my bachelor's. Nearly three years prior to this visit, we had spent a week traversing and exploring every nook and cranny of the city. The city's colonial past consists of the occupation by the Dutch, the French, and the British. Its grid-iron pattern, as seen now, traces its origin back to the late-17th to the early-18th century; the French implemented it, though it was initially planned by the Dutch. The city was divided into two quarters, the French and the Indian (or Tamil) quarters, which were called the White and Black towns, respectively; a racial divide established by the French to separate the areas occupied by them from the native ones. To execute the separation, they built the Grand Canal, severing the town into two quarters. The French Quarter was confined by the man-made Grand Canal to the west and the Bay of Bengal to the east.

The many colonial-era buildings occupying apparently larger plots and painted with pastel shades of yellow, blue, grey, brown, and white, the beautiful array of the openings, columns, railings, and the parapets in those buildings' elevations, the street names starting with '*Rue*' (a French word meaning street), trees edging the boulevards, and flowering plants, in particular bougainvillea, spreading out on the compound walls, the paved pathways and neatly maintained streets, the general silence felt in the neighbourhood, various government offices and important public buildings, high-end establishments including boutiques and heritage hotels, people seeming to be tourists walking and cycling along the pedestrian-friendly streets, the ones seeking spiritual awakening in the Sri Aurobindo Ashram, and women wearing white shirts and *khaki* shorts riding their bicycles, all of which are characteristic of the French quarter. In stark contrast was the hustle and bustle of the Indian quarter, featuring congested and poorly maintained streets, closely packed buildings, several notable Tamil mansions, heavy commercial and business activities, wholesale markets, too much traffic and a near absence of pedestrian paths, and people mostly seeming to be natives.

Two of my friends from SPA were residents of Pondicherry, Rishie and Vigneswaran; the latter was a native as well. Being thoroughly familiar with the place, they became our 'local guides'. We walked along the promenade and had appetizers from the historically significant Le Café, located along the promenade lining the seafront. Strolling ahead, I sighted the prominent structures and landmarks along the streets, to mention a few, the Aayi Mandapam in the Bharati Park, the statue of Mahatma Gandhi, Sri Aurobindo Ashram and the French War Memorial; landmarks I had previously painted in watercolour on a large A0 sheet during my bachelor's studies. At the edge of the French Quarter, we crossed the Grand Canal, which looked contaminated then.

Upon reaching Vigneswaran's home, we all enjoyed a delicious lunch. With the sweet course, they served us *sharbat* too, the flavour of which was mind-blowing. On enquiring, his mother told us that they made it themselves. Post-lunch, everyone, including his family, paid a visit to his family-run food processing facility, only a little apart from their home. While bidding farewell, our hosts gifted us their best-selling products as a token of love. We set forth towards the beach and accessed it through a shortcut. That part of the beach was calm and clean. We dipped our feet in the waves that, little by little, wiped the sand off the shore. While walking along the beach, we picked up the seashells lying around, mostly of white colour. Sandy beaches are absent in the city of Pondicherry due to severe sea erosion. The seawall, consisting of granite boulders built along the shore, protects the city from coastal erosion. In the evening, we went to

Jawaharlal Nehru Street, a major commercial spot in Pondicherry.

Back at the camp, I remained uneasy about the window openings that sliced the darkness into rectangular patches. The strong winds that blew through them threw away the weight I had kept on the free end of the curtain. But I was determined neither to let loose the grasp on the blanket nor to open my eyes. I waited impatiently for the sun to rise. Luckily, sleep embraced me in a few minutes. And I had a sound sleep till the break of day.

In the morning, we vacated the Youth Camp for the town. Foreigners who have been living there for years were zipping around on their two-wheelers. One could sense the influence of foreign culture and lifestyle on the natives, too. At a junction, most of the local people were wearing T-shirts, shorts, hats, and sunglasses. Shopkeepers would talk to their customers in English or French, or whichever language was known or spoken by the latter. At a roadside stall, a shoemaker was selling custom-made footwear. Hiring two-wheelers from a nearby rental vehicle shop, we started our expedition to Auroville.

Auroville... I have been hearing this name ever since I joined my undergraduate programme. It was one of the many topics that came up in the casual and in-depth discussions with my friends and practicing architects. Some of my classmates and senior students had been there for the purposes of case studies, site studies for thesis, internships, and architectural practice. It is quite normal that the architecture and the way of living practiced there would influence those who are fed up with living in a world of confusion and chaos. Based on the firsthand accounts of people who had lived and worked there, I had already created a cognitive map of the city. Winding pathways, some without street lights, culverts, people speeding on rented bicycles and scooters along the unpaved pathways, lush green vegetation, experimental architectural works, the community living there including a sizeable foreign population, the unique socio-economic system that places collective good at the forefront, the financial system which discourages the use of cash, windows covered only with curtains, unsecured by the usual metal grills, the Mother, the Matrimandir wherein the ones meditating get to transcend themselves into another world.... and a lot more.

Auroville is referred to as 'the City of Dawn', derived from the French words *Aurore*, meaning dawn, and *Ville*, meaning city. It lies mostly in the state of Tamil Nadu, with a small portion falling in the UT of Puducherry. It is an experimental international township founded in the year 1968 by Mirra Alfassa, also known as The Mother. She was a French-born spiritual collaborator of the Indian scholar, revolutionary, and spiritual visionary Sri Aurobindo (Aravind Ghose). The Mother was entrusted with giving a concrete form to Sri Aurobindo's vision: the creation of a new world, a new humanity, and a new society expressing and embodying the new consciousness. His vision was manifested as the city of Auroville, though he had passed away one and a half decades prior to its founding. Both of them believed in the evolutionary processes happening on Earth and that the human race would be surpassed by a supramental species, a diviner race, for the arrival of which transitional beings in human form are necessary to establish suitable conditions.

The city is envisioned and modelled as an ideal universal city where people can live peacefully and harmoniously. It aims to project itself as a model of 'the city of the future' or 'the city the earth needs', with the ultimate purpose of realizing human unity. The master plan of the city, based on the concept of a galaxy, was formulated from the basic concept as sketched by The Mother in 1965. It was developed upon by the French architect Roger Anger.

Located at the centre of Auroville is the soul of the city, the *Matrimandir.* It sits on 'Peace', a large oval-shaped open area surrounded by a lake. The township radiates outwards from the lake, as four zones; namely Industrial, Cultural, Residential and International, to the North, Northeast, South (or Southwest) and West, respectively. They are the important aspects of the town's life as sketched by The Mother to fulfill the vision of making it a universal city. The city, with a diameter of five kilometres, is bound by a green belt consisting of forested areas, farms and sanctuaries with scattered settlements. Although designed for an ultimate population of 50,000, Auroville currently has about 3,300 permanent residents from 60 nations, most being Indian nationals. The township has since then been progressively developing and growing to fulfil its stated goals.

What I saw in Auroville was almost similar to the cognitive map I had made of it in advance. I felt happy to have come to Auroville, so that I can contribute more effectively to future discussions. In the interactive audio-visual room at the Visitors Centre, I listened to the founding of Auroville, a grand concept planned for the future. After having breakfast at the cafeteria, we went to various spots near the reception. Waiting under a shaded tree, I noticed an installation which made a chiming sound when the wind blew. Rishie told us that most of the sound installations that we would find in Auroville were designed by a group called '*Svaram*', who experiment with sounds and devise musical instruments and installations. Auroville also promotes various other innovative and eco-friendly products.

We could not access the *Matrimandir* as prior booking had to be done. The tickets to visit the Matrimandir were available for the following day only, and we were leaving for home that evening itself. Thus, the visit was called off, and I kept the ticket as a souvenir. We had to be content with its view from the vantage point to its south, named 'Matrimandir Viewing Point', which is a few minutes' walk in the shade from the Visitors Centre.

The *Matrimandir*, literally meaning 'Temple of the Mother', is a huge golden sphere, envisaged by the Mother as a place for trying to find one's consciousness. She has described it as the symbol of the divine's answer to man's aspiration for perfection, and as the central cohesive force for the growth of Auroville. The upper hemisphere of the Matrimandir has a spacious white-coloured Inner Chamber, with a luminescent pure crystal-glass globe at its centre. Meant for individual silent concentration, the Inner Chamber is devoid of any religious symbols or other imagery. The Mother did not want the new consciousness to become a new religion, as she knew that exclusion and division are the failures intrinsic to religions. Thus, Aurovilians are expected to lead a spiritual life, instead of a religious one. To the Southwest of the Matrimandir could be seen a raised marble-clad urn, which, on the inauguration of Auroville in 1968, was filled with soil brought from 124 nations from across the world and from 23 states of India, by the youth belonging to those places, proclaiming the birth of a new and experimental city, and of a new consciousness altogether.

The city of Pondicherry, laid out by the French colonialists in a strict grid-iron pattern, with two different zones for occupation by Indian and French citizens, was deliberately planned to be mutually exclusive in nature, in line with imperialist thinking. In sharp contrast, the universal city of Auroville, located a short distance from Pondicherry, has been inspired by the concept of a galaxy, with four zones radiating out from the core based on function rather than the fault lines created by caste, creed, political, regional or religious affiliations. It aims to achieve human unity and is inclusionary in nature. The beauty of our thoughts translates through noble designs into humble yet great spaces.

Leaving the Viewing Point, we proceeded to other areas of Auroville. Riding through the woody tracts, we stopped by the buildings that were architecturally unique, or the ones pointed out by Rishie, who had the experience of working there. The built forms demonstrated the experiments done with spaces, materials, colours, light, ventilation, and so on, and also the innovations introduced in various fields such as education, housing, group living, and sustainable building practices. There were some extraordinary school campuses, configured to connect and merge with nature. Auroville is one of the greatest opportunities for people who have creative, experimental, and sustainable ideas.

A silence—specifically, a pin-drop silence—was one noble quality I had found in most of Auroville. The idea behind Auroville and the way it has been articulated inspires anyone seeking silence and simplicity in their lives. Even though some areas seemed deserted and woody, with buildings scattered wide apart, chance encounters with Aurovilians or strangers does not feel frightening. The people residing there and those coming there are directed to abide by the general guidelines issued by Auroville. On our way to lunch, from a distance, I saw some familiar faces who were wearing colourful kurtas and printed baggy *harem* (or *Aladdin*) pants. Coming closer, we were surprised to identify each other. They were none other than my classmates in Bachelors who regularly go on trips. People might have experienced some moments in their lives which reinforce the saying, "It is such a small world".

Moving through the forest-like deserted environment, we came across '*Svaram*', where sound was being experimented with and engineered by musical enthusiasts. Their workshops for research, and their shop selling handmade musical instruments, were located on opposite sides of the road. Altogether, it looked like a guild of eminent craftsmen of earlier times. The finished works were exhibited in their shop and in the forecourt. I was filled with excitement as I examined instruments that produced such unique, unfamiliar, and unheard-of sounds. Inside the shop, they demonstrated a musical bed that could be used for music therapy. Lying on it, I could really sense the power of sound when various notes were being played. In a city that encourages silence, they proved that sound can be harnessed to achieve that very stillness. I moved around, seeing the displays and listening to the vibrations on the percussion instruments and the metallic ones. As I ran my fingers over the strings of an instrument I had never seen before, I felt myself begin to melt. It sounded as if water was dripping down, as beads would fall from a string. Each time I played it, the sound 'rained' through my mind, accompanied by flashes of spark and lightning.

18 BIENNALE AT FORT KOCHI

When we aspire to something sincerely, it will find its own way to us, as brilliant thinkers would say and also as experienced by all of us at least once in our lifetime. This happened between the Biennale and me.

Biennale is an Italian word meaning biennial or every other year. In art, it refers to a large-scale exhibition of international contemporary visual art, conducted every two years. The Kochi Biennale Foundation, with the support of the Government of Kerala, organized the first-ever Biennale in India, named the Kochi-Muziris Biennale (India), in the city of Kochi in Kerala, in 2012. The name of that Biennale has two place names: Kochi and Muziris, two trading hotspots on the historical world map. Kochi possesses an eventful history—ancient trade with the Arabs and Chinese; reign of the Rajahs of Cochin; colonial past influenced by the Portuguese, the Dutch and the British; and migration of other communities from different parts of India primarily for trade. Muziris was a vibrant ancient port with international trade links. A massive flood destroyed it in the 14th century. It was along the Malabar Coast, to the west of India. The site was identified to the north of Kochi, and excavations have been going on since then. It was the fall of Muziris that paved the way for the rise of Kochi as a port city and a major trading centre. The Biennale seeks to bring forth the cultural fusion and legacy of these two historic ports.

The Kochi-Muziris Biennale, now in its sixth edition and held in the same city, has become an international platform for art in India. Here, artists get to showcase their signature pieces of art on the large canvas of a coastal city to the world community. Moreover, they can connect with their fellow artistic figures to discuss the current trends in the world of art. Art acts as a powerful medium to reinvigorate the cultural links and exchanges that have existed since ancient times through economic activity of trading.

The third edition of the Kochi-Muziris Biennale was underway in 2016, during my tenure as an ad hoc professor at the College of Engineering Trivandrum (CET). Though different media covered the events, I always longed to see them in person. Due to various reasons, I missed the first two editions of the largest art exhibition in India. This time, I did not want to miss it at any cost. It was quite a coincidence that I came to know that our first-year students were planning a day's trip to the Biennale with their faculty. I, too, expressed my willingness to join the tribe. Discussions, permission letters, the long list of students, confirmation.... everything was readied within hours, and the journey was set in motion.

Thus, the long-awaited day, on the sixth of January 2017, started at 3 AM, when I got up, jolted awake by a threatening wake-up call. The daily route to my college appeared darker than ever, and the cool air of the winter month was piercing every pore of my clothing, and deep into my bones, taking advantage of my then slim physique. I reached the college well before the stipulated time and found a nice seat in the front row of the bus. My desire for sleep was shattered by some students who woke up for nature's call, howling and shouting at each other. Despite the interruptions, I managed capture some images that are iconic of the places we were passing through, like the industries of Kollam and the marvellous temples alongside the roads in Alleppey. Entry to Kochi was obvious to my visual and olfactory senses, even though the Corporation had been doing its level best.

Within less than an hour of entering Kochi, we greeted Fort Kochi, the host of the Biennale. It is located at the mouth of the Vembanad Lake, which flows into the Arabian Sea. The place derives its name from Fort Emmanuel, built by the Portuguese in this part of Kochi in 1503. Since we had arrived an hour prior to the entry hours for the Biennale, we set out to experience and associate ourselves with the setting of the venue beforehand. With the deep waters of the Arabian Sea, the slow-moving giant cargo ships floating on her waters, the huge trees shading the streets and squares, the way-side vendors, and the local residents, tourists and art enthusiasts seen along the streets, Fort Kochi was springing to life for the day's show. They were all ready to be captured by the shutterbugs. But life there was composed of numerous frames and a hundred different stories, rather than being made of individual, detached frames. While walking, memories from three years ago came to mind. Back then, I came here on a ferry after attending the Young Architects Fest 2014 held in Kochi.

The venues readied for the Biennale included existing art galleries, halls, public spaces, heritage buildings, and vacant structures like old warehouses that were spread across Fort Kochi, Mattancherry, and nearby areas. Wandering through Fort Kochi, one could find Biennale's on-street installations that served as the setting for countless interactions and events. While we were analyzing one such installation, there came a newlywed couple who found it ideal as a post-wedding photography destination. In a few seconds, a tourist guide halted there to provide a brief description to the foreign couple she had been guiding. She was talking about the difference between 'socialism' in Kerala and as seen elsewhere. The same installation turned into a selfie spot too, for those passing by. Thus, Fort Kochi became a laboratory of art, where even the layperson could experience and experiment with art in their own ways and means. Lost in thoughts about the installations, we lost our way in the maze of streets with changing cross-sections. Thankfully, some friendly passersby helped us find our way back to the main road.

We entered the St. Francis CSI Church, a 16th century structure that upholds its colonial legacy. It houses the tomb of the Portuguese explorer Vasco da Gama. Though he was originally buried here, his remains were subsequently relocated to Portugal. The space around the tomb was crowded with a large group of students from Tamil Nadu. I tried to have a look at his tomb, but could hardly see it. Giving them ample time to see the church and its special areas, I moved away from that crowd and sat on a bench. For a moment, while looking at the interior, I reminisced about my visits to churches in Delhi and the hill stations of Nainital, Lansdowne, and Dalhousie.

Post the visit to Fort Kochi's famed Kashi Cafe, we set foot in the Aspinwall House, the prime Biennale venue. The artworks displayed there included different media, such as paintings, sculptures, photographs, movies, installations, music, and dance. Those exhibits ranged from stationary pieces to ones set in motion. It is no exaggeration if one finds the creator(s) behind the creation of every artwork to be multi-talented and a polymath. They possessed the skills of an artist, an architect, an engineer, and a performer, and an understanding of philosophy, psychology, and other disciplines which come into play to convey the concept behind their respective works to the spectators and critics. The works exhibited there were awe-inspiring. However, a few were disappointing. They evoked mixed emotions among onlookers, mostly disgust and fear, because of their upsetting way of presentation.

The art critics or the viewers were worth mentioning. Some were patiently sitting on the benches kept in front of the artwork and analyzing the works for long hours. Some just had a look at all the works and found much time to admire only the works that had interested them, to figure out what the creator had meant and to find the link between the brief given and its outcome, a category to which I also belonged. And some others came there just to see what was going on inside. Interestingly, while I was analyzing a work, a young man who happened to step into the main venue asked me what 'Biennale' was.

Through engaging works of art, artists brought art to the doorstep of the common man. Until this initiative, many might never have entered a gallery or exhibition space, known the value and utility of art, or understood that they could enjoy it in its authentic forms and forums. Thus, the Art Fraternity's Biennale was metamorphosed into a People's Biennale in Fort Kochi. Events like talks, workshops, and seminars held alongside the exhibition, encouraged public discourse on topics impacting art and society.

Despite hosting the exhibition and its offshoots, Aspinwall House also offered a great opportunity to explore its architecture, like other venues and designed spaces of architectural significance within that urban framework. We shared our views and feedback on the works seen until then during break time for snacks and lunch. For the first time, I had fish from outside of my home to associate myself 'deeply' with the culture and cuisine of Fort Kochi, and to absorb the Biennale in its fullest sense.

Of all the venues into which we had stepped, I found Pepper House to be an interesting spot, where I tried to see all the spaces shown in the popular Malayalam movie, Premam, and was trying to match the scenes of the movie with the actual setting seen there. I even took a photo sitting on the same bench where the protagonists in the film met each other, which was quite interesting to recreate. Greenix, Map Project Space and David Hall were other venues which also marked our presence.

Exhausted after a long day of walking and hopping between venues, we all wanted to wind down with some evening tea. While searching for a tea shop by the beach, we found a crowd near the Vasco da Gama Square behind the Bastion Bungalow (which was built by the Dutch in 1667 on the remnants of Fort Emmanuel). In the centre of the crowd, a few traditional artists were engaged in *Kalamezhuthu*, putting fine colours in powder form on the sandy ground. They were handling the colours carefully, so that they would not get blown away by the cool evening breeze from the sea.

From Fort Kochi and the Biennale, I took home some beautiful memories and a handful of inspirational ideas and thoughts to encourage myself to expand my knowledge in art. Some frames remained the same in the evening, too. With the deep waters of the Arabian Sea and the slow-moving giant cargo ships floating on her waters, the huge trees shading the streets and squares, the way-side vendors, and the local residents, tourists and art enthusiasts seen along the streets, Fort Kochi was drawing the curtains for the day's show. Besides these scenes, there were some new ones too. Places are like that; some elements in them remain the same, some are erased, and some are added in layers of time. Most of these frames were captured by the lens. While most others were captured deep within my mind and heart as interrelated frames, crafting a meaningful and thoughtful work of art.

19 MY SOUL WAS IN THE ABODE OF CLOUDS

I have always looked at northeastern India with awe. Though there is considerable diversity across the country, the people and culture of the Northeast are strikingly different from those of other regions in India. My school textbooks, images, newspaper clippings, and television documentaries had all familiarized me with the rich culture unique to the Northeastern region, which comprises eight states. I found the land and life there to be incredible and special enough to be explored in the future. Luckily, I had many opportunities to get to know the region better—the Children's Day celebrations at National Bal Bhavan, the Children's camp in Chhattisgarh, and, yes, my B. Arch classmate Lalmawipuiakhiangte (whom we called 'Puia' for short) from Mizoram. The closest connection was formed through our studio project in M. Arch at SPA, titled 'The Cultural Landscape of Shillong', for which an entire semester was earmarked.

One of our professors warned us about heavy rains in Shillong and advised us to opt for other sites for our on-site studies to avoid worrying about the climatic conditions. Since most of us had not been to the Northeast, we unanimously voted for Shillong; even if nature were to turn unfriendly and throw tantrums to keep us away. As the visit approached, I began the countdown and made arrangements, keeping the high likelihood of rain in mind.

The geographical aspects of Meghalaya, of which Shillong is the capital, were presented to us by an expert in geography well in advance. While she was skipping through the slides, something caught my eye—the natural formations inside the caves, rising from the floor and hanging from the roof. They are called stalagmites and stalactites, respectively. They are formed of calcium salts deposited by dripping water. These caves are located mainly in limestone formations. She said that one could find these natural formations in the caves of Meghalaya, including the Mawsmai Cave near Cherrapunji. Randomly, I made a wish right at that moment: "I want to see those natural formations within the Mawsmai cave".

During our visit, the railway network did not extend to many parts of the Northeast, owing to the hilly terrain. Thus, we had to get down at Guwahati railway station in Assam. The happiest part was that I could see the mighty Brahmaputra when our train crossed the river along the rail-cum-road bridge of Saraighat. Spending a night and another day in Guwahati, we started off on our two-and-a-half-hour journey to Shillong in hired cars. The entry to Shillong from Guwahati showcases how the Northeast stays unique and different from the rest of India; people, food, villages, waterfalls, soaring mountains, and so on and so forth. The entire landscape and the way of life were so impressive that the journey left me with many unforgettable images. There was a risk of landslides on the way, but fortunately, we had reached Shillong a few days before such events occurred on the same route, subsequently blocking the passage of many vehicles. Before reaching Shillong, we stopped by Umiam Lake.

As our professor told us, the city was under intermittent rain. From day one of the study, we were either holding umbrellas or wearing raincoats, facing difficulty in recording the collected information. The soaked clothes took days to dry. However, I thoroughly enjoyed the rain and the happiest times I spent in Shillong—the moments at the Golf Course lawns, Ward's Lake, Tea Pot restaurant, Police Bazar, Don Bosco Museum, Laban, Mawlynrei village, among others, still remain, and will stay green forever in my mind.

Shillong lies on the Shillong Plateau, surrounded by the Garo, Khasi, and Jaintia Hills to the west, north, and south, respectively. Meghalaya is inhabited predominantly by three tribal communities: Khasi, Garo, and Jaintia. The Khasis are the prime inhabitants of Shillong. Descendants of people from the neighbouring states and Bangladesh make up the diverse population of Shillong, which has a sizeable population of *Bengali*-speakers.

The businesses in the markets, wayside hotels, and homesteads and farms in the rural areas, run or managed by women, reinforced what I had known from a young age about the matrilineal system followed by the Khasis. Even the surnames of people whom we talked to in Shillong were derived from their mothers' names. The Khasi women were seen wearing their traditional dresses—*Jainsem* and *Jainkup*—be it in offices or in other public places. At a hotel in a village, hip-hop music was being played on a tape recorder, while the owner was preparing lunch for us. She was wearing a *Jainkup* and had a sling bag as an extra accessory, worn across her body to safeguard her earnings; a look typical of bold Khasi women.

At the end of our studies, we planned a one-day trip to Cherrapunji. I was so excited that morning to visit my dream destination in Meghalaya. The locations we covered that day included the mystical sacred groves in Mawphlang and its surrounding meadows, Cherrapunji, and the David Scott Memorial. The next in line was the one on my bucket list—the Mawsmai cave, located around 60 kilometres to the southwest of

Shillong, in Sohra, near Cherrapunji, in the East Khasi Hills. It is known as *Krem Mawsmai*: *Krem* meaning cave in the local Khasi language. Only 150 metres inside the subterranean cave is open to the public.

All of us got the tickets and walked towards the cave. The crowd was larger than I had expected, and some of my friends started sharing their fears of crowds and stories of past stampedes. We entered the cave that was totally soaked through. Water kept on dripping from the ceiling of the cave, forming puddles on the floor. The floor and ceiling were highly uneven, making exploration difficult. Families flocked in, and some mothers, while guiding their kids, were rushing into the cave and jostling others. They pushed me as well, which was more than enough to frighten me given the stories my friends had told. I imagined a scenario where I tripped on the wet floor and was trampled by the crowd. The mere thought of it shook me. "Enough! What if this nightmare comes true!? What if I get trapped?! Let me escape from this cave, however amazing it is! I am going back!" Just a moment of fear, and that was it. More than the actual risk of falling, I was dealing with a fear of falling.

I let my fear pull me back from achieving my wish to go deeper into the cave. Though so close to my dream of completing the trail inside the cave, I retreated after covering a few steps from the entry. I let my dreams succumb to my fears for the first time ever. While waiting outside, my friends and teachers, who had gone inside the cave, came out through its exit and shared their experiences of exploring it. I felt ashamed and disheartened for what I did not do, which I could otherwise do with ease and confidence. I told myself, "I must come here, and I certainly will!" Every time I thought of Mawsmai, I regretted it. Days and months passed by, making new wishes on top of the old ones like the accretions of calcium salts deposited by the dripping water inside the cave; yet the longing to enter Mawsmai Cave lay fresh, deep beneath the layers of other wishes made subsequently.

The time was ripe to visit Mawsmai Cave one and a half years later. As soon as I landed at the Delhi Airport for my Convocation in January, a Professor from the College of Engineering Trivandrum called and asked me if I was interested in going with the B. Arch students on an All India Educational Tour in April, to Meghalaya and Bhutan. I had no words to express my readiness other than to nod and say, "Yes! I am in!" My heart filled with joy when I saw Mawsmai in the tour itinerary. I kept the trip a surprise for my friends at the SPA, who had seen me standing unhappily outside that cave.

It was a long and arduous journey: first from Thiruvananthapuram to Chennai by train, and from there to Guwahati by flight. From Guwahati, we proceeded to Shillong that very night by road. Upon arriving at the Police Bazar at midnight, I recognized the places I had traversed several months ago. The next day, we headed to Nongriat village, about sixty kilometres to the southwest of Shillong. We got off at Tyrna village, from where we trekked to Nongriat village, which did not have vehicular access. The only way to reach the village was by walking more than a kilometre—just keeping on walking until we finally reached it!

After the trek along a winding pathway, we went down 3600 steps along the steep mountain. Then we carefully walked along two swaying, narrow cable bridges laid across beautiful rivers that were dotted with pebbles and reflecting the blue sky and the greenery around. Again, we had to negotiate the ups and downs of several hills. While we were gasping and panting, a few local residents were hurrying to the village. They were carrying construction materials and other essentials in cone-shaped woven baskets that were resting on their backs and fastened to their heads. The Khasis living here are experts in undertaking such laborious treks through the hilly terrain—ascending and descending hills of varying heights, and crossing rivers—all of which have eventually become a part of their daily life.

Finally, all these strenuous efforts came to fruition when we reached Nongriat village to find the man-made living-root bridges. The village has a single living-root bridge and a double-decker living root bridge, which is built at two levels. Such living root bridges can be found in other areas of Meghalaya as well, to connect the banks of a river or two hillsides. The giant roots growing above the ground (aerial roots) of the Rubber tree (Ficus Elastica) have been skilfully interwoven to build a 'natural transportation infrastructure', serving generations of villagers. Looking at the river, the rock masses seen underneath it and to both its sides, the trees on either bank of the river, and the bridge—all gave the impression of having evolved organically into a single entity. The Khasis place great importance on nature, their way of living being at one with it. Religious beliefs, customs, and traditions have been attached to natural features to protect and conserve them, an example being the sacred groves in Mawphlang. Even the names of many villages and settlements in Meghalaya are derived from or related to natural elements or features.

Tourists and trekkers coming to experience authentic village life here would soon be witnessing an 'urbanized village'. New construction materials and techniques, so far alien to the village, were being introduced to provide facilities such as homestays, changing the local architecture. This would only aid in severing the Khasis from their age-old practices, which undoubtedly were in harmony with nature and sustainable. Just as we decided to leave, a team of senior citizens was approaching the village to stay there overnight.

We retraced the same winding and tiresome path. Like many others, I was literally gasping for breath and low on energy while climbing up the 3600 steps back. Since everyone was exhausted, the organizing team considered removing Mawsmai Cave from the tour itinerary. I despaired and felt sorry for myself, as the close opportunity to see the cave just slipped through my fingers. Disappointment overwhelmed me, and I sat sadly in the vehicle as we drove back to Shillong.

To my surprise, I saw my fortune popping up again at the diversion point, when our vehicles were directed towards Mawsmai Cave! It was the plan of the student coordinator, who wanted to give all of us a surprise. I was overjoyed to see the stone erections at the entrance gateway to the cave.

Hurray! I swiftly collected the tickets and ran to the cave. A few among us were hesitant to enter the cave, out of fear or for other reasons, and yet I inspired them to go inside. As the cave was ill-lit, I switched on the small, cute torch that my father had gifted me to guide my path and that of those near me. Instead of instilling fear in my students by telling them stories of stampedes and other mishaps, I inspired them to move forward carefully by watching their steps and minding their heads while squeezing and crawling through the narrow passages. I enjoyed being inside the cave to the fullest, and watched with awe the unique formations inside the limestone cave, including the stalagmites and stalactites, the fossils, the dripping water, and also the 'sun roof'-like dolines lighting and ventilating the cave from above. The interplay of water and limestone, like artisans working together, has created plenty of natural installations in the cave interiors that might get transformed with the passage of time. As soon as I reached the exit, I jumped in excitement and captured the moment in a photograph. It was a moment of transition, from abandoning my dream to achieving it.

I felt that I had left my soul in Meghalaya one and a half years back, only to get it back now. "Mawsmai, you made my day! And you taught me a lesson for the rest of my life."—The things that we believe to be and seem to be challenging are really not so. They just threaten us with a veil of risk and probably fear, but nothing else and nothing more. Just unveil it and enjoy the exceptional moments that life brings to us. We will praise ourselves for what we have done and not for what we had dreamt of, and be proud of ourselves for our accomplishments, however comfortable or complicated they may be!

That night, we camped in tents alongside the Umngot River, in Dawki, a town bordering Bangladesh. I wished for a peaceful New Year to commence the next fine day, as it was the occasion of *Vishu* (a harvest festival of Kerala), which in that year had coincided with Good Friday. That morning, we visited the Mawlynnong village, which was selected as 'Asia's cleanest village' by Discover India magazine. The next day, at Police Bazaar in Shillong, I saw my dear friend Puia, after two years, by coincidence. And on the very same day, even in a weak health condition, on account of the consequences of the trek to Nongriat village, I did the adventurous sport of zip-lining at Mawkdok in Sohra. I credit it all to the 'Mawsmai effect'!

20 HAPPINESS IS TRULY A PLACE

My relationship with Bhutan started on my day of admission at the School of Planning and Architecture, New Delhi, in July 2014. I was at UCO Bank, next to my college, to remit the tuition fees. While standing in the queue, I noticed a pleasant-looking girl doing her transaction at the cash counter. The bank employee asked her to give an exact change of five rupees. She searched her wallet, but to no avail. Seeing this, I gave her a five-rupee coin. Hesitantly, yet thankfully, she took it and said that she would give it back soon. Her name was Ngawang: she had come all the way from Bhutan to study at SPA. She shared with me her first-hand information which gave me a sense of what to expect from the college and hostel life over the next two years. Since all of us were in a hurry to finish the admission procedures, we wrapped up the conversation in a few minutes.

Having completed the administrative procedures for joining the school, the next step was to move into my allotted hostel room. While transferring my belongings to the hostel, I saw three girls celebrating their friend's birthday. They were hurrying through the passageways, screaming with joy. One of them happened to bump into me. She said sorry and continued to be a part of the celebration. At a later date, I came to know that they were also from Bhutan. And Ngawang was one of the many students from Bhutan enrolled in the various courses at SPA. Education and people-to-people ties are among the binding forces that have been strengthening India-Bhutan ties.

Not even on a single occasion, to my knowledge, have I seen the students from Bhutan in a state of distress or tension during the days in Delhi. They seemed to enjoy every millionth of a second of their lives, truly living in the moment. I never asked them the reason for their happiness; it felt like an unnecessary question to ask, given our busy schedules. Chance encounters with a happy Ngawang in the common areas of the School always cheered me. When I saw her at the college two and a half years later, in January 2017, she reminded me, with her characteristic innocent smile, that she still owed me five rupees! But she never knew that I owed her far more than she owed me—the friendly attitude, the smiles, and the pleasant greetings she had extended to me.

The reason for the Bhutanese students' happiness remained a mystery to me until I reached Bhutan as part of an educational tour from CET, where I was working as a faculty member. After touring Meghalaya in the Northeast of India, we proceeded to the landlocked Himalayan Kingdom of Bhutan. It was a journey that took seven hours by train from Guwahati in Assam to New Alipurduar in West Bengal. And from there, by road, to Phuentsholing (or Phuntsholing), a town in Bhutan bordering the Indian town of Jaigaon in West Bengal.

Winter was just over on this side of the subcontinent, paving the way for spring. Still, the chill of the cold season lingered around. It was getting cold at night, and I fell asleep. On reaching the Indo-Bhutan border, those who were awake screamed, "Wake up! We are at the border! Yeah....Over there is Bhutan!" Hearing this, I woke up and looked through the window. Wow! A lovely place....and a brilliant-looking entry gateway, adorned with a riot of colours. That is the Bhutan Gate separating the two countries. It was just a sample of what was yet to be seen in the small hill country.

We checked into a hotel in Phuentsholing. Post breakfast the next day, the first mission was to secure entry into the country officially. That day, we were literally stuck at the Immigration Office in Phuentsholing. Administering and managing the huge number of foreign nationals seeking entry into their land was a herculean task for the officials. The dressing style of the staff at the office and of the natives is worth mentioning. They were wearing traditional dresses, namely *gho* (a knee-length robe for men) and *kira* (an ankle-length dress for women), conforming to the dress code for Bhutanese citizens. And the foreigners, of which we were a part, were in an attire alien to our own respective cultures! Those awaiting clearance were sitting idle on the porch under the severity of the sun. Some people ran out of energy, some moved hastily, and others engaged in heated arguments within the office. Having had enough of seeing and experiencing the effects of the long wait, some of us thought of having a sneak peek at the town and having refreshments.

Because we crossed the border at night, I could not see the transition from India to Bhutan. Phuentsholing, which acts as a gateway to Bhutan from India, is a permeable border where people and goods of both countries can move freely for various purposes, including cross-border trade and tourism. Though geographically, the towns of Phuentsholing and Jaigaon on either side of the border are the same entity, they were drastically different, as a consequence of their inclusion in different polities. The town in Bhutan, located to the north of the Bhutan Gate, was orderly and well-articulated. The town in India, located to the south of the Bhutan Gate, featured honks, noise, and dust, imparting a feeling of chaos and helplessness. A country's laws, their societal implementation and enforcement, and citizen acceptance all shape the culture followed within a political boundary. A nation functions well when the trio of rules, rights, and responsibilities runs in unison and harmony. Disorder and misrule are the outcomes when and where rules are violated, rights are well fought for, and responsibilities are forgotten.

To cross the road in Phuentsholing, we made sure that there were no vehicles in the vicinity, but the traffic police stopped us and directed us to follow the zebra line, and so we did. In Bhutan, even without signals for pedestrians, those drivers, a greater number being ladies, would patiently wait for even the slowest pedestrian to reach the other side, and we could see them always smiling.... their eyes telling us, 'Take your time'. Bhutan, being a small nation with a manageable population, implements rules effectively, and the citizens take pride in abiding by them. There, vehicles do not honk. There, hotels never serve stale food that looks 'older' than the guests; otherwise, the establishments would face closure and penalties. Instead, they prepare every order from scratch. So it is probable that we might get our food with a delay. Still, Maggi arrives in just two minutes, as advertised.

We entered a supermarket and went through the products on display. The designs, including those of dragons, on different articles looked similar to the ones commonly seen in Asian countries, especially East and Southeast Asia. There were products that were imported from India as well, as India has been a major trading partner of Bhutan. Indian currency is accepted in Bhutan as legal tender, and the Bhutanese *ngultrum* (monetary unit) is at par with the Indian *rupee.* It was interesting to note that the taglines of various products and souvenirs sold there read, '*Happiness is Bhutan*'!

Bhutan adopted happiness as a state policy in the latter half of the 20th century, through the concept of Gross National Happiness (GNH), and was the first country to do so. The GNH policy, which was constitutionalized, has four pillars spread over nine domains and 33 indicators. In GNH, the economy is just one among the nine domains and not an absolute factor. Traditional economic indicators like Gross National Product (GNP) and Gross Domestic Product (GDP) instead measure the progress of a nation solely based on the economic growth and development it achieves. The GNH measures the quality of the nation across four pillars: promotion of sustainable development, preservation and promotion of cultural values, conservation of the natural environment, and establishment of good governance. The initiatives Bhutan has been taking with GNH as the guiding philosophy bear fruitful results for nature as well. It is evident from both the high percentage of forested area and Bhutan's feat as the first carbon-negative country in the world. Bhutan, the 'Kingdom of Happiness', teaches us that happiness is a pursuit not of selfishness, but of selflessness, and that happiness is found when the collective good is prioritized above personal wants of individuals, and that happiness is to be valued more than anything else, be it material or monetary.

One day spent in Phuentsholing was an introductory yet all-inclusive session on Bhutan. Eager to learn more about Bhutan, we set out for Thimphu late in the evening.

Bhutan is a landlocked country on the eastern ridges of the Himalayas. It is bounded by the Tibetan Plateau to the north and the Duars plain to the south. The Duars plains are the alluvial floodplains falling in India and Bhutan, and lying between the Himalayas and the Brahmaputra basin. Phuentsholing is located in the Duars Plain. The adverse conditions in the cold, rugged Great Himalayan region, and the malarial tracts bordering the Duars Plains limit most of the settlements to the fertile Lesser Himalayan valleys of the Central and Western region, and the Southwestern region of the country; Punakha, Thimphu, and Paro being some examples. Due to the geographical proximity, Bhutan has been influenced by Tibet, located to its north. The name 'Bhutan' is the Anglicized version of the Sanskrit '*Bhotanta*', meaning the end of Tibet, as Bhutan occupies the southern end of the Tibetan plateau. The populace, as we see now in Bhutan, are the descendants of immigrants from the nearby regions of Tibet, Nepal, and India.

Bhutan's official language is *Dzongkha*. Since Bhutan became a unified state in the first half of the 17th century, it has been known as *Druk Yul* in *Dzongkha*. *Druk* means the Thunder Dragon from Bhutanese mythology, and *Druk Yul* means the Land or the Kingdom of *Druk*. The national flag of Bhutan features the *Druk* in black and white colours. The *Druk* is set against a background divided diagonally into a yellow upper triangle and an orange lower triangle, signifying the equal importance given to the civic and monastic traditions of the Kingdom, respectively. Most of the Bhutanese follow Buddhism, in particular the *Drukpa Kagyu* branch of Tibetan Buddhism, the 'spiritual heritage' of the country.

Prayer flags were a common sight in Bhutan, often found near temples, homes, bridges, and along the slopes of hills. These flags in red, blue, yellow, green, and white colours represent the five elements of nature. In Buddhism, these colours, if placed in harmony, are believed to be good for the mind and the body. The belief is that when the flag flutters, it releases the prayer printed on it into the air, which carries it to the heavens. Strong winds helps them flutter more, sanctifying the air, and bringing good fortune and longevity to those who erected them. Thus, they are positioned along the locations that receive the maximum winds, in particular, hillsides. There are several types of prayer flags, including *Lung Dhar*, which are horizontally strung, *Darchog*, which are vertically strung onto poles, and *Mani*, which are raised after the death of a person. They dot the rugged landscape, fluttering like feathers, and set the breathtaking views of the hill country in motion.

Another religious symbol seen in Bhutan was the prayer wheel—a hollow metal cylinder over which is wound a scroll of prayer. The act of whirling or turning the wheel by hand equals the recital of that prayer. I saw them for the first time in McLeod Ganj, a suburb of Dharamshala in Himachal Pradesh, which also has a significant Tibetan population.

*Chorten*s are also ubiquitous in Bhutan. As Buddhism spread to other parts of the world from India, architectural forms similar to the Buddhist stupas developed in different regions under different names, such as *Chorten*s in areas with Tibetan influence and *Pagoda*s in East Asia. Worshippers pray and circumambulate Chortens, which vary greatly in size.

Thimphu, the capital and largest city of Bhutan, sits in a beautiful valley, the bird's-eye view of which was captured on the way to the Buddha Dordenma statue. The buildings in the city are painted with a rich palette of colours, and all seem like the output from the same mould. The building regulations in Bhutan mandate that new buildings incorporate traditional architectural elements, such as the use of multi-coloured wood in the front elevation, small arched windows, and a sloping roof. Iconic structures such as the administrative and nodal buildings stand out in the context. The official royal residence of the present King is called the Samteling Palace.

In almost every place we had been to, be it an office, a shop, a hotel, or a restaurant, I found the photo of the royal family of Bhutan, framed and fixed onto the wall. It was with great respect and pride that everyone told us that those were the photos of the rulers of Bhutan. That shows how revered the royals have been in the minds of the citizens. Bhutan has been following a constitutional monarchy since 2008. It marked a shift from the absolute monarchy, wherein the king was called the *Druk Gyalpo*, meaning Thunder Dragon King. In the new system, the king is the titular head of state, and the Prime Minister is the head of the government. The monarch of Bhutan leads by example and acts as a role model for the citizens. Their citizen-friendly measures are rooted in the concept of GNH; their way of living suggests to the citizens what to follow.

In the city of Thimphu, we could see several types of structures. The National Memorial Chorten is a religious structure built in 1974 in memory of the third monarch, King Jigme Dorji Wangchuk. Located on a ridge, the Changangkha Lhakhang is a temple complex dating back to the 12th century, which is visited by parents with their newborns or young children to seek the blessings of the deity. The Folk Heritage Museum offered a wealth of information, displaying diverse aspects of Bhutanese culture, such as traditional architecture and everyday artefacts.

We moved to Punakha, the old capital of Bhutan, a three-hour drive from Thimphu. There, we went to the Druk Wangyal Chortens in the strategic Dochu La Pass. Numbering 108, these were built to honour the Bhutanese soldiers who had lost their lives in the 2003 battle with the Assamese insurgents from India. In the afternoon, we crossed Bhutan's longest suspension bridge, which is laid across the Pho Chhu River. The intermittent light showers made the day even colder. After lunch, we reached the Pungthang Dechen Phodrang (Palace of Great Happiness or bliss) or the Punakha Dzong, a monastery built in the 17th century. It is a marvellous and majestic structure located at the confluence of two rivers, the Mo Chhu and the Pho Chhu, to its west and east, respectively. From the confluence, they flow together as Puna Tsang Chhu or the Sankosh River, which crosses the border, and ultimately become one with the Brahmaputra River. Unlike the other areas seen so far in Bhutan, Punakha was comparatively low-lying, bounded by mountains, with rivers cutting through the plains. The Dzong was accessed through a covered wooden bridge across the Mo Chhu River.

Graced by the Kingdom's two major lifelines and adorned with the violet blooms of Jacaranda trees dotting the river banks, the Dzong was a perfect blend of strength and splendour.

It was a huge monastery, looking like a fort, with towering exterior walls, a massive entry door, temples, a lot of chambers for administrative purposes, residences for monks, and several courtyards. The high exterior stone masonry walls, sloping inwards, were painted white, their upper bands painted in red ochre and accented with wooden openings. Not only has the structure stood the test of time, but it has also withstood disasters like recurrent fires and floods, and earthquakes. Massive internal timber columns and beams in huge galleries are a defining feature of the structures here. In timber roofing, the traditional construction did not make use of nails or iron bars, and for roof covering, shingles and stones were used, which are being replaced by modern construction materials. Until 1955, when Punakha was the capital of Bhutan, the Punakha Dzong acted as the administrative centre and the seat of the government of Bhutan. The Dzong still functions as the administrative centre of the district of Punakha, and it has been the venue for the coronation ceremonies of the kings of Bhutan.

Dzong means a fortress-monastery. In the past, it served as a stronghold against enemies while carrying out the vital religious, military, political, economic, administrative, and social functions of a district. They now undertake administrative and monastic functions. The one at Punakha is situated on a plain, surrounded on three sides by rivers, unlike the others, which occupy prominent locations in the hills. The unexpected rain that showered down while I was walking from the exit of the Dzong to the wooden bridge inspired me to write on the postcards I had bought in Thimphu. On one, I wrote, "It's all berries and blossoms everywhere!"

The next day was the most thrilling and the most awaited one:

the trip to the Tiger's Nest in Paro, in West Bhutan. The Taktsang Goemba (or Taktsang temple) or 'the Tiger's Nest' as it is widely called, has been attributed to the Indian yoga practitioner Guru Padmasambhava (Guru Rinpoche), who is believed to have visited Bhutan in the 8th century. It was a meditation cave, and later the monastery was built around it. In the morning, all of us set out on a two-hour journey to the Tiger's Nest, on the cliff-side of the upper Paro Valley. Standing at the foothills, I got a glimpse of the monastery toward which we were trekking. Seeing the monastery nestled along the rock face of a steep hill, I wondered how it was constructed; a question I kept on asking myself, especially whenever I encounter rock-cut architecture in such rugged landscapes.

Mules and natural hiking sticks were hired for climbing uphill in order to save energy for the rest of the trek. I got a 10-year-old mule named 'Rakpay'. There were a few temples en route. The soothing sound of the waterfalls and the general silence of the forest made me trek with a tranquil mind. Prayers were being offered by the fluttering coloured flags. More than a trek, the journey felt like a pilgrimage. The monastery, located uphill as seen through the pine forest, was astounding.

I bid farewell to Rakpay, who dropped me midway. Somehow, I hiked the remaining path with the help of my wooden hiking stick. Finally, I reached the Tiger's Nest, an accomplishment that reminded me of the movie Kung Fu Panda. I left my stick at the entrance and began exploring the temple complex. The balconies in the monastery provided unmatched, spectacular views of the valley below, clad in conifers and other vegetation. A foreign couple's guide very generously invited me to listen to his talk. After seeing all the spaces inside, I moved towards the last destination in the complex, the underground cave chamber where Guru Padmasambhava had meditated. The passage that led to the cave chamber was very narrow, much narrower than that of Mawsmai. However, I entered it by descending the rock-cut steps and a ladder.

Reaching the exit, I inhaled some fresh air at the cliffside. The serenity of the monastery also offered tranquillity to my mind. And I felt that my energy had doubled, giving me the assurance and confidence to climb down the hill. I grabbed my stick, which was kept at the entrance, and descended the steps as swiftly as an arrow. A slow-moving young man from Singapore told me he felt exhausted just watching me run. Replying with a smile, I continued to run, bouncing with every step. I took shortcuts that at first seemed like misleading pathways. I tried to hold on to the wild plants on the way, only to find that they were thorny, which mildly injured my fingers. Many a time, I was alone and about to fall, but my shoes gave me the grip needed to advance, and the stick acted as my companion and brake.

Finally, after all these adventures, I reached the downhill, a flat area surrounded by pines and dotted with apple trees bearing countless blossoms. There, I found a perfect rock on which to recline. I sat on it, looking higher upwards at the Tiger's Nest, and I lay down right there, fully stretched out, with my eyes closed and legs crossed, my head resting on my locked arms. For several minutes, I remained empty-minded, dreaming of nothing. I could feel happiness above and beyond, and I was taken to the extreme height of happiness; a state of bliss! In spite of the clouds turning black, showing signs of another shower, I remained calm. "Let it rain. I have a place underneath the rock-mass to hide." I realized happiness is a place, and for now, that place is this little rock piece in Bhutan!!!

21 THE DECCAN DIARIES

Can a hot and dry climate make someone feel 'cool'? Yes, the places on the Deccan plateau can. Even though I had been to various parts of the Deccan in the past, such as Gulbarga, Mysore, and Bengaluru, it was in fact the studio tour in March 2018 from the TKM College of Engineering, Kollam, which made the region so dear to me. We toured Chikmagalur (officially Chikkamagaluru), Hampi, Badami, and Bengaluru, all of which left a lasting impression on me. Among these, Hampi became my favourite, showcasing the vividness of the plateau, sculpted by gifted hands, dynasty after dynasty.

A senior professor read out the rules of the trip to everyone assembled in front of the college before boarding the bus. One rule was to travel in groups with a faculty member as the team lead, resulting in six such teams. As the journey progressed, this rule got violated, that too in the first destination of Chikmagalur in Karnataka. Thus, the team leads formed a group themselves and started moving together, which turned out to be the most exciting part of the trip.

From Hassan, it took almost an hour by road to reach Chikmagalur. It was around noon when we headed from the camp house to the hills in jeeps for trekking. Chikmagalur (or

Chikkamagaluru) is a hill station on the Deccan plateau, at the foothills of the Western Ghats. The hilltop where we had reached first provided a panoramic view of the hill ranges, valleys, forests and the coffee plantations of Chikmagalur, the highlight of which was the cool and strong winds that kept blowing atop the hill. And the sky was clear, with a radiant glow from the afternoon sun.

We drove further uphill to reach the highest peak in the state of Karnataka, the Mullayanagiri Peak, with an elevation of 6300 feet above sea level. There was a temple on its summit, to be accessed by climbing a series of seemingly endless steps starting from the drop-off point for vehicles at the base of the hill. Climbing steps is apparently a good measure of our courage, the internal driver, and our physical health, the carrier. It is the synergy of courage and physical health that carries us to new heights. At every pause during the trek, I took a deep breath and looked back to see how far I had come. The sun was turning red by the time I had covered three-fourths of the distance. Finally, I conquered the long flight of more than four hundred steps. Some of us came up, and some remained at the parking lot itself. Giving up climbing the steps would have been a substantial loss. The view from there was so beautiful that we spent that evening on the premises of the temple, until the setting sun hid behind the hills, painting hues of red onto the canvas of the sky. Cameras could only capture our silhouettes against the warm colours spread out in the sky. Descending the steps, we rode back to our camp house located downhill, where evening tea and snacks awaited us. Late in the evening, we moved to the next location, Hospet.

I woke up to a busy morning at Hospet (or Hosapete). Bullock carts, a rarity in most of Kerala, were visible alongside the road. A morning tea with my team at a local shop was the perfect start to the day. After refreshing at our hotel, we set off to the next destination on the itinerary, Hampi, about thirteen kilometres away.

Hampi was the capital of the erstwhile Vijayanagara Empire for around 200 years, starting from the 14th century (1336 AD). Following the Battle of Talikota in 1565, between the Vijayanagara Empire and the coalition of Sultanates, the city was deliberately brought to ruin through massive destruction and subsequent abandonment. Though largely in ruins, Hampi continues to fascinate everyone with its grandeur, and it is a UNESCO World Heritage Site under the name 'Group of Monuments at Hampi'. The architectural landscape on the rocky or hilly terrain of Hampi includes temples, shrines, mandapas, water structures like water tanks and baths, royal structures, forts, markets, and much more; most of which now lie in ruins.

As we were nearing Hampi, I felt as though the colours around us were gradually disappearing, except for the shades of yellow ochre that became concentrated, with patches of greenery spotted here and there. While standing at the intersection of Hampi Street and Hampi Bazaar Street, we were clueless about where to begin. So, we thought of exploring the various spots in the historic city at random, based on convenience and choice. Our students, eager to cover all of Hampi, could be seen speeding by on bicycles every now and then. Being positioned near the Virupaksha Temple, it was naturally our first stop.

Virupaksha Temple, a massive feat in stone, is a living monument where deities and devotees have been exchanging their blessings and offerings, respectively, for several centuries. It is at the western end of the broad Hampi Bazaar Street, also known as Chariot Street or Virupaksha Temple Road. The *gopuram* of this East-facing Saivite temple is a striking feature that serves as a landmark for orientation among the surrounding structures in Hampi. A large wooden chariot stood in front of the *gopuram*. On entering the *gopuram*, we reach a court, to the extreme West of which were located two pillared halls (*mandapams*); the one to the North is the *Kalyana mandapam*, and the one to the South is the Krishna Deva Raya Coronation mandapam, with its richly sculpted plinth and pillars. While walking through the court, I could see a hill to the south of the temple complex. Owing to the rising temperature outside, we sought refuge in a shaded area near the Krishna Deva Raya Coronation mandapam. Krishna Deva Raya was the third monarch of the Tuluva dynasty, who ruled over the Vijayanagara Empire in the early 16th century.

Moving further, a smaller *gopuram* leads us to another court where the main temple is located. This court houses several subsidiary, smaller shrines. The exterior of the main temple, including its walls and pillars, has been exquisitely and profusely carved. The plinth and pillars of the mandapa facing the main temple have been beautifully sculpted. This time, we sought refuge in the shade of a pavilion that covered the northern and southern sides of the *pradakshinapatha.* Sitting there, we shared our thoughts and knowledge about Hampi, its history and heritage.

Another smaller *gopuram* opened to the northern side, leading to the Manmatha Tank, which was surrounded by *mandapa*s. Approximately 200 metres to the north of the temple complex flows the Tungabhadra River. Some structures in this temple complex were already in a damaged state.

Upon exiting the temple complex, we headed south and climbed the hill that was earlier seen from inside the temple. With the sun positioned right overhead, this portion of Hampi felt like one of the driest places on earth! It was Hemakuta Hill, a barren granite slope dotted with monuments such as temples, water cisterns, and mandapas, as well as huge boulders and rock masses scattered all over it. The group of temples seen here belongs to a much earlier period than the others in Hampi, probably from the

9th to the early 14th centuries. The Shri Krishna Swami temple is located further south of Hemakuta Hill.

Lost in the beauty of Hemakuta Hill, we almost forgot about our lunch. However, upon realizing it, the hunt for an eatery kicked off. We started walking along the narrow, winding streets in the residential cluster at the northeastern corner of the Virupaksha temple complex, sheltered from the direct glare of the sun. In one lane, we found a welcoming hotel where we had our food served on a low table, and ourselves seated on cushions laid on the floor. After a heavy meal, everyone took a brief nap there. Leaving the hotel, we walked along the high embankment built at the edge of the Tungabhadra River.

The Tungabhadra was flowing towards the east, embracing and moistening the land it touched. This area was comparatively greener, lush with plantains, coconut trees, and other vegetation. Granite boulders scattered all along the river resembled beads on a broken string. The hillocks on the other side of the river appeared to be simple piles of boulders of varying sizes and shapes, interspersed with grass. The boulders in the river include sculpted ones, including one that bears the figure of a bull. Our walk ended at River Road, which provides access to the Virupaksha Temple to the south and the Tungabhadra Ghats to the north. Vendors had set up small stalls on carts parked parallel to River Road, along its northern side. The ghats have stepped access from various points along the River Road. We descended through one of them to reach the waterfront.

Boat service, called the Hampi-Kishkindha ferry, was available from the ferry point at the western end of the ghats. A few passengers were seen getting off a small boat at the ferry after their trek to the other bank of the river. Some coracle boats (traditional round boats) with their steersmen (navigators), who seemed to be local residents, were ready to ferry people across the river. A coconut seller had set up his thatched-roof stall near the ferry, beside a big boulder, facing the river. There was a stone mandapa near the ferry, accessed through several flights of steps down the River Road, and another mandapa located halfway along the steps. Innocent-looking monkeys were hopping on the steps in the ghats and climbing the trees near the road. I had also seen some of them inside the Virupaksha Temple. The evening sun appeared like a chrome yellow spot in the sky, with a red-orange halo around it. I savoured the evening spent at the riverside: the stone mandapas, the rock masses, hillocks, and the green patches that thrived wherever tiny pockets of soil were available on the rocky surfaces.

We changed our location to the ghats near the ferry. An elephant walked along River Road, guided by its mahouts. A few minutes later, it was brought to the ghats for a bath. The elephant slowly and carefully descended the steps as we watched its graceful gait in awe. I captured photo after photo of the scene. Four of our team members asked for a photo with the elephant in the background and the four of them in the foreground.

Halfway through, I sensed something wrong with the elephant's movement through the lens. Yes! It was not slowly descending the steps anymore; it was indeed dashing down the steps, towards us, spontaneously! In no time, I sent out alarms, and in a fraction of a second, the tetrad dispersed in whichever directions possible, like the sudden sparks of a cracker. To avoid being trampled by the elephant, the 'photographer' too fled from the scene and took refuge behind a pillar in the mandapa nearby. Phew! I breathed a sigh of relief, having found a safe zone to escape into. After clearing the site, the elephant slowed down at the ghats and gently immersed itself in the river. I guess it was teasing us. Ensuring that the elephant had calmed down, those who had scattered because of its antics gathered back at the mandapa and shared their tales of escape. I showed them the photos I took a few moments ago; they were funnier than any animated movie I have ever seen. Seeing them, we burst out laughing. That was the most interesting part of our first day in Hampi.

Back at the hotel after dinner, we gathered on the lawn, and each one contributed their share of creepy stories—an inevitable ingredient of meet-ups with friends. As we listened to them, instead of getting scared, we found ourselves laughing throughout the story session. Laughingly, we entered the lift to go to our rooms on the upper floors. When it landed on the first floor, an employee of the hotel got in. The lift door closed, and after a fine takeoff, the lift stopped suddenly, and the lights inside it flickered. And that was enough to scare even the bravest among us. Out of fear, we started to sweat and shiver, and were all set to scream aloud for help. Thankfully, before we ventured into such extreme measures, a timely response came, and we reached the landing safely. That night, I prayed to get rid of nightmares.

The next day, at Hampi, we changed our plan. It is nearly impossible to see the whole of Hampi on foot. And wandering around on foot, under the scorching sun, in a semi-arid climate, is exhausting. So, the ideal solution was to hire a bicycle; it was cheap, eco-friendly, and saved both time and energy. I took a Ladybird bicycle, which resembled the one I had at home. Once everyone got the bicycles of their size and choice, we started our ride along the highway-like, wide, old Hampi Bazaar Street. A hat, loose clothes, sunscreen, and a bottle of water are must-haves for a Hampi visit during summer.

As we rode along Hampi Bazaar Street, I realized that one of the best ways to explore Hampi was by riding bicycles. The previous day, when moving on foot, I missed seeing or simply could not enjoy certain places, structures, and sights. But, this day, I could enjoy them from a bicycle—the pillared stone market buildings on both sides of the Street; the long stretch of coconut trees standing behind those market buildings; the cows, oxen and horses loafing around in the streets; the *mandapa*s; and many flights of steps and gigantic boulders of the hills seen at the Eastern end of the Street.

Parking our bicycles near the *mandapa*s, we ascended the stone-faced steps near the *Nandi* shrine (monolithic bull) at the eastern end of Hampi Bazaar Street. Upon reaching the shrine uphill, I turned around to behold a grand view of one of the main centres of the city: the Virupaksha temple, at the Western end of the Street, the boulders at the Hemakuta Hill to its Southwest, and the *mandapa*s near where I was standing. On climbing the steps further up, I halted at the landings in between the flights of steps and looked back, and found the grandeur of that view getting multiplied. I stopped at a *mandapa*, called the Santebeedi viewpoint, at the end of the long series of steps, and rested there for a few minutes. The winds that blew through its pillars took away the weariness of the hot and dry region accumulated till then in my body. For one last time, I looked back, and I glimpsed the 'royal' vista of the old capital of the Vijayanagara Empire. I wondered, "How lively this place must have been in its heyday!" The memoirs of foreign travellers who visited Hampi in its golden years mentioned the city.

From the Santebeedi viewpoint onwards, the trek is risky owing to the discontinuous steps. Moving ahead, the pathway becomes irregular and unpredictable, bordered by huge shrubs with thorn-like branches, and strewn with stones and boulders of different shapes. We were actually climbing along the contours of what is one of the highest points in Hampi, the *Matanga Parvata* (Hill). Descending the hill, I caught a grand view of the Achyutaraya temple and market complex, located to the East, in a valley, surrounded by hillocks, including *Matanga* Hill. The roofline of the temple seemed to imitate the skyline as defined by the hills surrounding it. In fact, the built forms of Hampi brilliantly blend with their surroundings. The place looked deserted, but for a few visitors, including a solo woman traveller. Going down the broken and uneven stone pathway, we reached the entry to the Achyutaraya temple complex.

Achyutaraya was the fourth monarch of the Tuluva dynasty that ruled Vijayanagara in the 16th century. Dedicated to Lord *Vishnu*, Achyutaraya Temple faces North, unlike most others that face East. In the entire complex, the temple enclosure is to the extreme south, and to its north is the pillared marketplace on both sides of the broad road, at the northern end of which is seen a *pushkarani* (ceremonial tank). The Tungabhadra sits a little apart, to the north of it, beyond which is seen the Hill of Anjanadri Betta or Kishkindha, believed to be the birthplace of Lord Hanuman. The structures in the temple complex were mostly in ruins, some strengthened and supported by buttresses added at a later time. Still, they had not lost their grandeur completely, as was obvious from the temple complex set within a rectangular courtyard, the broad road with the long stretch of markets, exquisite carvings and sculptures on the stone plinth, pillars and walls of the temple, and the ones on the entry *Gopurams*, among other things. They reveal the skill of craftsmen who lived and worked about seven hundred years ago. The floor of one structure was covered in sand. So I had to lift my legs each time they sank deep into the sand. After exploring the temple and its premises, everyone assembled in front of the temple and had a quick view of the market street, and together, we walked back to the bicycle park.

By noon, we had depleted our energy and water. Bottles of water, once opened, got emptied in a flash. Hampi was too vast to be covered in its entirety in just two days. Realizing that a heavy lunch would eat away our precious time remaining in Hampi, we skipped it for the day to go for something lighter. Along Hampi Bazaar Street, old women were selling buttermilk kept in earthen pots. I had buttermilk and bananas from one of them. A recommendation from a teammate about another old lady selling a different and better flavour of buttermilk drew us to her cart. I gave it a try, and on sipping it, my body instantly cooled down and got energized as well. Buttermilk apparently helps quench thirst, especially during field visits and tours in arid areas. I had plenty of buttermilk and bananas, without knowing the 'after-effects' of this combination, specifically during summer. In relaxed mode, I started cycling again, with a cool mind and body.

We turned northeast from Hampi Bazaar Street and followed a path through plantain groves to reach the riverside. We were carrying our bicycles when the pathway turned into stone-faced steps bordered by rock masses. At the last lap of the pathway, we had to pass through a natural cave named Kampa-Bhupa's path, the exit of which provided access to the riverside.

This place, in the valley formed by the *Rishyamukha* Hill to the north and the *Matanga* Hill to the south, is called the *Chakratirtha* (meaning sacred whirlpool), where the Tungabhadra changes her direction and flows northwards and becomes narrower. People regard it as the holiest bathing spot in the river. The *mandapa* that sits on the southern side is accessed by ghats formed of cut stone blocks. We safely parked our bicycles in the shade of a small thatched structure at the ghats. The riverside had a few temples, including the Kodandarama Temple. From this part of the river, one could access both the Achyutaraya temple complex and the Vitthala Temple.

The eastern side of the bend in the river had a blanket of weeds. The rocky outcrops on both sides of the Tungabhadra and the boulders dispersed on her, bejewelled and beautified her. Coracles and boats were moored near the flat, rocky base of the riverbank, where a few coracles were laid upside down to dry, and a few boats lay abandoned. The rock surface featured several sculptures and relief works.

While enjoying the surrounding visual delight, my abdomen started giving distress signals- Yes! The 'after-effects' of the buttermilk-banana combination were coming into play. My teammates suggested certain remedies that had helped them in the past in similar situations. I tried each of those following their step-by-step instructions, all of which were less intrusive. I stopped drinking water, remained still, and lay on my stomach underneath the thatched roof where we had parked our bicycles. Seeing that I was resting and feeling better, they handed over their bicycle keys to me and went to explore the area.

Distress signals popped up again, as all the remedies which had initially seemed helpful subsequently proved futile. That was when I found my own solution—simply reaching a nearby washroom along Hampi Bazaar Street, about a kilometre away. I called my team members who were enjoying the beauty of the riverside. When I informed them of my plan, they tried to stop me. Ignoring their calls to stay and suggestions to try some more remedies, I rushed to grab my bicycle. But I had the bad luck to have a few identical keys. As I could not recognize my bicycle's key, I tried some permutations and combinations. Finally, I found a key that matched another bicycle. Leaving the other keys nearby, I unlocked that bicycle and carried it while ascending the rock-cut steps. My friends were not ready to let me leave alone. Partway there, two of them came running after me with my bicycle. Since I was running short of time, I waved at them and told them to go back. After reaching the plain area, I put the bicycle down to ride.

Unfortunately, the bicycle I was carrying did not have a bell, and the seat was a bit too high for me. Even so, given my critical condition, those were just luxuries. There was no time left to replace the bicycle, and I was already too far from my team. I knew I could not cover that distance again. Bad luck was haunting me, yet I had no time to blame it. I summoned all the courage I could gather and was determined to ride it anyway. From there on, I sped through Hampi Bazaar Street, navigating heavy traffic, to reach the 'pay and use' public utility on the right. Dashing into the complex, I miraculously escaped the dog resting in front of it, and leaned the bicycle against the compound wall. I called out to the keeper, "I'll pay you on my way out!". Before he could give me an answer, I vanished. And that was it! Problem solved! I came out peacefully with a smile on my face, paid the keeper, took my bicycle, and rode it back humming my favourite songs.

I rejoined my team, which had been awaiting me at the entrance to the facility. The never-ending thirst for water urged us to find a cold drinks shop. Juice and water were of little help in keeping us hydrated in a hot season. Still, we had to settle for them, as the only other option was buttermilk. We retraced the same path to the riverside and passed by the Kodandarama temple, ghats, *mandapa* and other structures on the way to reach the next spot, the Vitthala temple, located to the northeast of the Achyutaraya temple complex.

The Vitthala temple, dedicated to Lord *Krishna*, is set within a rectangular enclosure which also houses other subsidiary shrines and mandapas. *Gopuram*s to the east, south, and north provide entry into the complex. The market streets are located to the north and southeast of the temple. Another temple is located at the end of the northern market street. The *pushkarani* was a little apart, to the southeast of the temple. Buggy vehicles were plying along the market streets, carrying tourists. Cattle were also moving along the same route. We entered the temple complex from the eastern *gopuram*.

A stone chariot representing the *Garuda* shrine is found at the entrance court of the temple, to its east. This structure has become one symbol of Hampi. Though in ruins, the Vitthala

Temple retained most of its original features. Some structures that were facing the threat of collapse had buttresses and support measures. Apart from the siting, layout and overall structure of the temple complex, I was awestruck by the artworks; such was the beauty of the sculptures and relief works. They were so elegantly handcrafted that they still continue to inspire those who arrive here. We moved around the temple and seated ourselves on the seating provided on the northern side of the *Ardhamandapa*, facing an old champak with new leaves and flowers. The tree also looked like a work of art, like an extension of the heavily sculpted built structure.

There are some commonalities between the Virupaksha, Achyutaraya, and Vitthala temples. They belong to the structures of the sacred centre, sited on the banks of the Tungabhadra River, which comprises mostly older temples and markets. The temples here are part of a large complex. Each comprises temples for principal deities and subsidiary shrines, confined within an enclosure entered through *gopuram*s, besides having pillared market streets and a *pushkarani*.

Having taken enough rest, we were ready to move to other locations in the city. Due to time constraints, our final destination in Hampi was the Queen's Bath, which is located in the royal centre, about 5.5 kilometres to the south of the Vitthala temple. Outside the temple, vendors were selling water and ice cream. Carrying bottles of chilled water on our bicycles, we rode along the Village Road to the east of the temple. Cycling through the cultivated areas and past two herds of goats at different spots along the road, I could really enjoy the beauty of rural life. In no time, we had to enter the busier zones of Hampi to reach the royal centre. Vibrant colours returned as we traversed the busy thoroughfares. The royal centre of the city is located to the south of the sacred centre. It is where the structures related to the royals are found, including palaces, ceremonial structures like halls and platforms, temples, water infrastructure like water tanks and aqueducts, granaries, elephant stables, etc. Most of the structures over there were in ruins. The entrance gate to the Queen's Bath was already closed by the time we arrived. Tired of riding, we sat beneath the shade of a nearby tree.

Darkness slowly enveloped Hampi as we rode 3.5 kilometres northwest, back toward Hampi Bazaar Street. We handed over our bicycles to their owner and arrived at the intersection of Hampi Street and Hampi Bazaar Street, where everyone was to assemble. While boarding the bus, I waved goodbye to Hampi. The darkness of that night was slowly bleeding into the yellow ochre colour of the city. Yet, I was sure that the blend of these two would produce shades of green, symbolizing new beginnings, growth, serenity, renewal, abundance, joy, and coolness. Stay green, Hampi!

Every place has something to tell us, which remains unexplored until we go in search of it. I continue to travel far beyond my home, finding and creating places of rootedness. Yet, I realize that the ultimate place of rootedness that I want to cherish and revisit is my mind itself, which is the treasure trove and the perennial wellspring of all my wonderful memories.

ABOUT THE AUTHOR

Jessin Kabir is a conservation architect by profession, and a writer and artist by passion. She did her schooling in Trivandrum, at Darsana Higher Secondary School and at Cotton Hill Government Girls' Higher Secondary School. After graduating with a Bachelor of Architecture from the College of Engineering Trivandrum (CET), Kerala, in 2014, she completed her Master's in Architecture with specialization in Architectural Conservation at the School of Planning and Architecture (SPA), New Delhi, in 2016, where she was awarded the Gold Medal. She has served as an Assistant Professor (Ad hoc) within the Department of Architecture at both the College of Engineering Trivandrum (CET) and TKM College of Engineering, Kollam. An artist at heart, she has received several accolades, both at the state and national levels. She is a recipient of the National Bal Shree Award for Creative Arts in 2005 from Dr A.P.J. Abdul Kalam, the then President of India. Various regional-language periodicals, including journals and newspapers, have published her artistic and literary works. *Places of Rootedness* is her debut book.

9 789357 779500

Printed at Repro India Ltd.